AF496509

The Young Cricketer

Ray Illingworth

The Young Cricketer

Stanley Paul/London

STANLEY PAUL & CO LTD
3 Fitzroy Square, London W1

An imprint of the Hutchinson Publishing Group

London Melbourne Sydney Auckland
Wellington Johannesburg Cape Town
and agencies throughout the world

First published July 1972
Second impression March 1974

© Ray Illingworth 1972

This book has been set in Times type, printed in Great Britain
on antique wove paper by Anchor Press, and
bound by William Brendon, both of Tiptree, Essex

ISBN 0 09 111450 0

Contents

Illustrations

Foreword

I have purposefully done a fair amount of name-dropping in the pages which follow and I think this gives a clue to the type of book I have tried to write.

Since my earliest matches as a young boy in Yorkshire, I have read a lot of coaching manuals and I have found many of them dull and soulless, and far removed from the sweat and excitement of competitive cricket.

Therefore I have tried to look at the techniques of the game as reflected in some of today's great players—men like Boycott, Sobers, D'Oliveira, Ian Chappell, Knott and Snow.

The result is not a comprehensive guide to coaching and playing. Nevertheless, I hope I have produced a book which will both help the young cricketer on the field and give him a little inside information as he watches a Test match at Lord's, Headingley or wherever it may be.

I owe a number of people thanks, especially Deryk Brown of Hayter's sports agency for his help in preparing the text.

Raymond Illingworth

1

The Shot I Left at Home

When I first went to the nets at Headingley as a fourteen-year-old the coach there was Arthur Mitchell, the former Yorkshire and England batsman. He will always be remembered for scoring four successive centuries in 1933 and he was also one of the finest silly-point fieldsmen of all time. As a coach he was a gruff old stick and he didn't use two words when one would do.

'If they can't understand what I'm saying they're not going to play for Yorkshire anyway,' he would mutter. He was never flamboyant, always hard to please, and being coached by him was like playing in the middle. Once I became adventurous and tried a cut. 'You can leave that bloody shot at Farsley,' said Arthur, referring to the village between Leeds and Bradford where I come from.

His attitudes might sound hard but I'm sure they were the right ones. No coach should shower his charges with advice and be constantly correcting them. No young player should become obsessed with the techniques of the game. Obviously, if a lad is doing something horribly wrong he must be told about it. But I've always thought that the coach's main role was to observe, see what talents are there, and say: 'Have you ever thought about doing this?'

I always feel it is particularly dangerous for coaches to spend too much time changing the action of natural fast bowlers. If I come across a lad who has natural pace but a peculiar delivery action, I'm not tempted to start analysing him. I might advise him on what type of ball to bowl but that would be all.

A talented young player called David Pickles came to York-shire with genuine pace and a 'wrong' action. He was coached so much that he lost some of his pace and never lived up to his promise.

Mike Procter (Gloucestershire and South Africa) is a coach's nightmare . . . and he can be a batsman's as well. He is a quickie who bowls off the wrong foot. At the moment the ball leaves his hand his right foot is ahead of his left which is com-pletely skew-wiff for a right-arm bowler. Froggie Thompson, a character with a liking for natty waistcoats who played against England in Australia in 1970–1, is the same.

Naturally I wouldn't advise anyone to try to bowl off the wrong foot. All I am saying is that natural ability and instincts are very important to a young cricketer and he should never be coached too intensely.

Peter Loader (Surrey and England) was all arms when he ran up to the wicket, and is another good example. Bill Bowes, a former England fast bowler and now an astute com-mentator on the game, said that no one could reach the top with an action like that. Yet Loader was the best new-ball bowler I have ever seen—and he is competing with some distinguished names. He could make that ball move in circles.

An up-and-coming batsman needs a little more help than the young bowler—he has his grip, stance and a whole range of strokes to worry about. The bowler, once his run-up is func-tioning well and he knows what he is trying to bowl, must help himself to a large extent.

Even so the coach must advise his batsman with discretion. Nothing is more likely to dampen a youngster's enthusiasm in his formative years than to be corrected for pulling a ball from outside his off stump. Let him enjoy the feel of striking the ball. Encourage him to play his strokes, because that, after all, is what batting should be about. Too many lads are taught too soon the defensive straight bat.

As a youngster grows up he should still be allowed to go on hitting the ball, but if he has difficulty in playing a certain type of delivery, that is the moment to help him. After that it is up to him to practise it.

You cannot manufacture a breed of player, at least it shouldn't happen. Everyone is different. The bat can be held differently, the feet may move slightly differently, even the head can be sometimes held differently.

Bob Barber, the Warwickshire and England left-handed batsman, was an example of what I call natural ability. He had this unorthodox streak in his play. He played a long way from his body, the bat angled for the ball to go through gully, but he was a wonderful striker of the ball for all that. If textbook instruction had been forced upon him in his younger days, we might never have enjoyed his dashing range of shots.

I know some people consider Colin Milburn, with his heavyweight punching, to be an example of the untouched player. But to me Colin is reasonably correct in his technique. He certainly pulled the ball better than most because he was so strong at, generally speaking, he struck the ball in the right direction.

Jim Parks (Sussex, Somerset and England) is another who may look wrong by orthodox standards. He does stand square, but if you watch him closely you will see that at the moment of impact he is fairly correct. Immediately he starts to play a shot, he gets his left shoulder round. It is a case of standing comfortably as far as he is concerned and adapting to the need of the particular stroke.

Clive Inman, a former colleague at Leicestershire, is a little unorthodox yet he may not appear so from the edge. It is only when you bowl at him that you realise this.

I can bowl to Inman, pitching just outside his leg stump, and he'll still hit it through the covers. He gets really inside the ball and hits it through the off-side.

Arthur Mitchell told me not to play the cut and some coach probably told a young Denis Compton not to play the sweep.

Compton was so good in his heyday 25 years ago that he was able to invent a stroke of his own. Colin Cowdrey is a more recent exponent of the sweep. He plays a particularly delicate one, swinging the ball round so far that sometimes it looks as though the ball will finish at third man instead of fine leg.

Personally, I often think that the sweep is a dangerous shot and not worth the candle. But if any player feels sufficiently confident to play for it, fair enough . . . provided the state of the game is right.

Anyone who is hoping to get to the top in a particular sport would be foolish not to be coached while he is still young. There is invariably something, however small, that can be picked up and improved pretty quickly.

Nothing, though, can replace enthusiasm and practice. The best way to learn to play cricket is to play it. Play it and enjoy it. The lad who is going to get most out of the game is the one who tries to play it every night of the week if he can. This keenness must apply to every facet of the game.

When I was playing my first cricket during the 1939–45 war the parks and open spaces didn't often get cut because there was little petrol for mowing. But that didn't stop the lads in our district from preparing their own pitch. We called it the Wreck. We dug it up, bought seed and relaid it and kept it in trim with one hand-mower and a pair of shears. One night disaster struck. A herd of cows strayed on to our precious wicket. The farmer drove them off, but not before they had churned up the whole area.

We had to spend most of our pocket money on levelling the pitch again, but then we would go to almost any length to stage our game.

I still watch the occasional match at Farsley or at Pudsey St. Lawrence, which is just up the road. The youngsters there still get a good grounding in the game, and especially from the present coach, Michael Fearnley. Also they have the great advantage of being able to mix in with players of county and near-county standard. The way to the top is still as straightforward as ever: a really promising youngster will work his way into the first team in his mid-teens and be recommended to the Yorkshire nets.

One thing that did distress me on the occasions when I recently watched Farsley was the quality of some of the batting. Often it seemed that if the batsmen blocked two balls on the trot he inevitably had a monstrous heave at the third. He did not appear to be able to increase the pace of his innings by using textbook shots. I think this applies to much of club cricket in the seventies.

I can remember a number of occasions in my day when Farsley began disastrously yet rallied by playing what I would call good cricket, and I can't help recalling one which gave me considerable pleasure. On one famous day our opponents were Lidget Green. I took a single off the first ball of the innings and then watched while Bill Copson, the former Derbyshire and England quickie, did the hat-trick that over. Each ball pitched a shade outside off-stump, each nipped back just enough. Then Gordon Barker, later of Essex, and I put on 150 and Farsley finished at 211 for seven.

I know one becomes nostalgic about memories like this and they become embellished (though the figures in this case are right!). But I wonder whether young league players of today can build an innings as surely and successfully as my generation could.

I think it is instructive that, as far as I can see from the records, scores in the Bradford League are lower than they were 20 years ago although the batsmen have just as much time. We used to play to an innings limit of two and a half hours, which often meant only 32 or 34 eight-ball overs. Now the league limit is 50 six-ball overs, more in terms of balls. Add to this that few sides seem to have a slow left-armer—an essential in my day—and I find it hard to believe that the batting is as good as ever.

EQUIPMENT

Look after your equipment and you'll be a better player because of it. Cricket can be so much a question of mind over matter, especially when you are young, that the moral advantage of looking clean and tidy is not to be overlooked. If you don't have a long-suffering mother, an obliging girl-friend, or a first-class laundry, there is only one thing for it—you will have to do your own washing!

Boots need careful attention. I know it can be difficult and expensive for parents whose lads are just taking up cricket because they will have to buy a new pair of boots every year. The lad will probably be pushing for a new kind of batting glove or for his own pads. He'd be better advised to have a pair of boots which fit and not try to squeeze into last year's size. The same goes for flannels—a pair which fit are more important than some status symbol to impress the rest of the team.

Considering the amount of time a county player spends on his feet from May to the start of September, I'm surprised there isn't more foot trouble in the game. Perhaps the reason is that most of us are generous with the talc or foot powder and inspect our boots regularly.

On the question of owning your pads, batting gloves and various types of sweater, it is necessary to strike a sensible balance. I know it's nice to own your own pads but if you are a slow left-armer who bats number eleven for the school third eleven it probably just isn't worth the money.

This doesn't mean that you should wait until the eighth wicket falls and then start searching furiously in the team bag for pads and emerge with something ridiculously ill-fitting. Plan in advance. That way you can be well equipped without spending unnecessary money.

But I would advise anyone who takes the game at all seriously to buy himself a bat. Whether it has a long handle or a short handle is usually a question of trial and error, and weight

Test match action against India at Lord's in 1971. Top right, a cover drive with a good follow-through; left, a hook, for which I have stepped well inside the line of the ball, and below, a sweep: note the downward movement of the hands and arms to keep the ball on the floor.

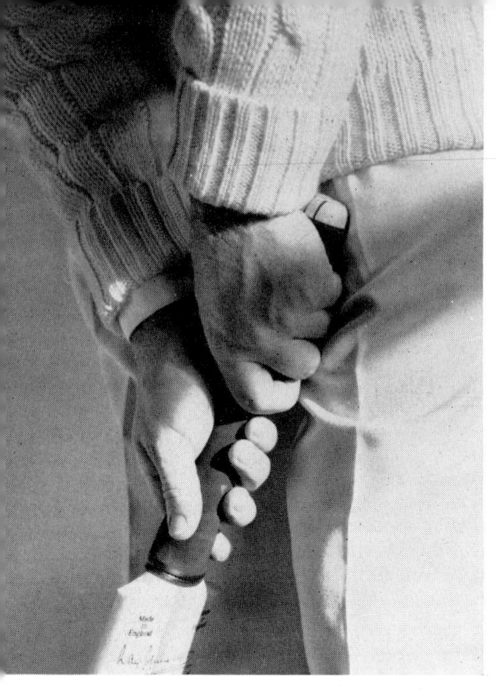 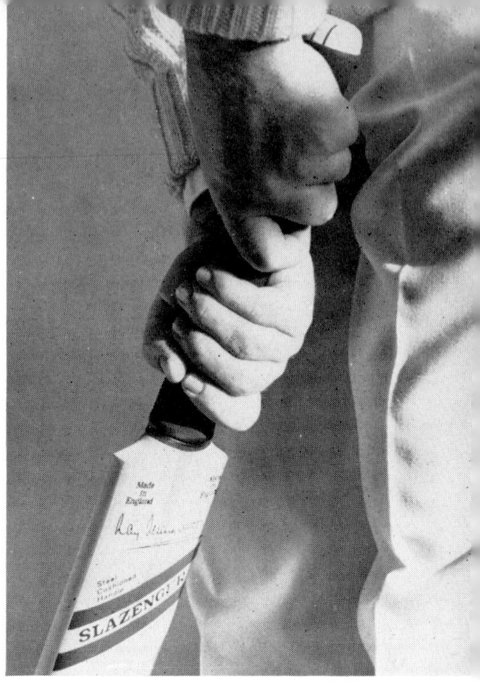

The correct grip on the bat (top left) and the bottom-hand grip (top right) in which the right hand has been pushed too far round the front of the handle. My two off-spin grips: one with the seam (bottom left) and one with the fingers going across it.

and size are other matters which only the individual can decide himself. When most boys have a new bat they proceed to oil it three times a week for a month, which achieves nothing save making a mess on the kitchen floor. This is excessive. A thin coating of linseed oil, perhaps after the bat has been sand-papered, and then a repeat a few days later, is enough in the initial stages.

Gloves—whether your own or the team's—need careful attention. Some prefer the gauntlet type, some those which leave the palm open. Whichever you choose, remember that a poor pair can cost you a chipped or broken bone and quite easily half a season's cricket.

The abdominal protector—or 'box', as everyone calls it—is a must. Never, ever, bat without one, however slow and inviting the bowler may appear. And I would strongly advise all those transferring from school to club cricket to wear a thigh pad when they are likely to come up against genuine fast bowling.

One final word from Arthur Mitchell. I remember him saying that if Doug Padgett and I didn't play for England, it would be his fault. We both did, although neither of us would have thought for a moment of blaming Arthur if we hadn't.

Don't lean heavily on your coach or blame him when things go wrong. He will help you all he can but he is not there to play your game for you. In the end it is your talent, sweat and luck which will take those wickets or score those runs, which will see you playing village green cricket on Sundays or playing at Lord's or Headingley. Cricket is the greatest team game, yet it is intensely personal at the same time. That is one of its beauties.

B

2
Batting

Walk to the wicket, don't slouch. Walk there as though you intend to score runs, a lot of them. The first ball is a hummer which flicks the edge of your bat, misses your stumps by a fraction and dollies to the wicketkeeper who drops it . . . Do not start knocking at the knees. Your luck is in, get your nose down and play an innings.

Batting is 75 per cent skill and techniques and 25 per cent self-confidence, application and guts. I cannot offer individual advice to young players who feel they lack some of that 25 per cent; I can try to console them by saying that confidence usually comes with the years. Even the best players have their crises—and it is not only the sixth-former who becomes depressed when he starts off the season, nought, nought and one.

CONFIDENCE

I think I can best illustrate the importance of confidence in batting by pointing out how often a batsman improves when he is promoted in the order. It happened to John Steele, who plays with me at Leicester. During the 1970 season he was going in at number eight and nine. With only the ten and jack to come, he was tending to play careless shots in an attempt to score quick runs.

Also, there was the psychological factor—no one was expecting him to score runs, therefore his attitude was naturally not the same as a number one batsman.

The next season we made him into an opener and he was a different batsman. He averaged more than 35 and had an agreeably small number of failures. Obviously this was partly a case of natural ability being allowed to emerge but confidence had a lot to do with it.

My own experience is a case in point. In 30 Tests before I became England captain my batting average was 16. In my first 26 Tests as captain my average was about 38. I made no changes in technique to account for this difference and I suppose my figures as captain ought, in fact, to have been that little bit worse because then I was cracking on to 40 and not as nippy as I was.

No, I was batting better than ever because I enjoyed the responsibilities of being captain and because I was settled in the order at number six (or sometimes seven) instead of the nine spot which I had previously occupied. The frailty of some of our earlier batting helped me in a curious way—for the first time in my career I was *expected* to get runs and people looked to me as a batsman.

Some cricketers have that gift of rising to the occasion. Basil D'Oliveira is one. In county matches he often looks an ordinary player; in Test matches he frequently came up with a big score and had a knack of breaking annoying stands with his swing bowling.

On the other hand, there are players who fail at crucial moments. Don Kenyon, now a Test selector, used to score bags of runs for Worcestershire and flop in the England side. Dennis Amiss and Keith Fletcher are two who did not score the runs they should have done in Tests although both have now demonstrated they can cope with the big occasion.

Schoolboys will have similar ups-and-downs. One of the beauties of cricket, especially at junior level, is the unpredictability of personal performance. With the right attitude, a boy of average ability can knuckle down to it and often score more runs than a more talented player. No youngster should walk on the field with an inferiority complex.

KNOWING YOUR LIMITATIONS

If I could give the aspiring batsman only one piece of advice it would be 'always play within your limitations'. By all means experiment in the nets with tricky shots you are trying to master, such as the late cut or the sweep; in fact, you *must* experiment otherwise your game will become sterile. In time you may feel confident enough to play these shots in the middle.

Meanwhile, play within your limitations. . . . You may have seen Geoff Boycott hook a bouncer for six on television but don't mindlessly try to copy him if you find the ball coming at you between the eyes.

What you perhaps didn't realise was that Boycott, a master batsman, had been playing Tests for six or seven years before he began playing the hook shot with any confidence.

I agree that the bouncer is an extreme example. The same reservations apply to a more straightforward shot like the off-drive. Tony Greig (Sussex and England) is a longshanks of about 6 ft 4 in and what a half-volley is to him is not a half-volley to all 5 ft 2 in of Harry Pilling, that splendid little Lancastrian batsman.

Time and again young batsmen are out quite needlessly because they aren't much taller than Pilling and they try to drive balls that only a Greig could drive. Stick to the right ball to drive and do not insist on trying to drive balls outside the range of your physical capability. This is just throwing away your wicket.

I am not suggesting boys should play defensively and be tied to their creases. I am saying that they and their coaches should work out what is worth risking one's wicket for and what is not. If a batsman can hook, pull, sweep and cut, I hope he will play all of these strokes whenever he can. If he cannot, say, sweep to save his life, he would be foolish to keep playing the shot.

THE BASICS

'Keep your eye on the ball' is such an elementary piece of advice but I won't apologise for repeating it here. It is essential yet so often ignored. Sometimes even in Test cricket you hear that the batsman was out when he 'lifted his head' which simply means that he didn't watch the ball. This may be permissible when you have a 'ton' on the board; if it happens short of that score you should rightly feel a first-class idiot.

The grip on the bat rarely presents problems, and if one adopts an orthodox stance it is odds on that one's grip will naturally be a correct one. As a rule the right-handed batsman will grip the bat near the top of the handle and the fingers will fall into place with the knuckles facing down the wicket. The right hand is placed lower down with the ends of the fingers facing down the wicket this time. There is a slight gap between hands.

Remember always that the left hand is the important one. It is a good idea when practising a forward defensive stroke to play it with the left hand alone and then you will see just how irrelevant the right hand is when you are putting your front foot down the wicket and playing defensively. In theory a top-class batsman can play an innings without a right hand and there are one or two pieces of cricketing folklore about a one-handed batsman bravely making runs. I can remember Len Hutton once doing it against the West Indies.

But I'm sure that even Hutton could not have done it with just his right hand.

The stance should come naturally too. For the right-handed batsman, the left shoulder points down the wicket, the left foot is a shade in front of the crease and parallel to it, and the right foot is a shade behind. The bat tucks in comfortably behind the right foot. For some reason young players often like to dig themselves a block hole which is an inch deep or more as soon as they arrive at the wicket, perhaps because they think it suggests they have come to stay. This is unnecessary.

As I mentioned earlier, Jim Parks has an open or two-eyed stance, as has Ajit Wadekar, the Indian captain. Laddie Outschoorn (Worcestershire) and that great accumulator of runs Kenny Barrington (Surrey) were two more whose front shoulder used to point to mid-wicket while the bowler ran up.

Who am I to say that they were wrong? Obviously I would correct any lads who were taking up the game if they started to look two-eyed down the wicket. But if I saw a lad of 14 or 15 making runs in colts matches I think I would be inclined to leave well alone. The important thing is that the stance should be sufficiently relaxed and the weight sufficiently evenly distributed for the batsman to go on either the front or back foot without difficulty. You should never lean backwards on to the bat and use it to stop you falling over. If you haven't the energy to stand up straight at the wicket it's as well to stay in the pavilion.

Your backlift is the foundation of most shots and therefore it is the essential that it is correct. 'Play with a straight bat' is not a rule invented by schoolmasters to make cricket a dull game. If your backlift is dead straight the bowler will see the full face of the bat; if it is dead square to the stumps the bowler will see only a side view of the bat. It doesn't take a great brain to work out that the straight bat has most chance of hitting the ball, and that the more crooked your shot, the more likely you are to miss completely.

The left hand must dominate the backlift. Try lifting the bat with both hands doing the work and you find that the right hand will drag the bat outside the off stump. You don't want this to happen. Hold the bat in only the left hand and let it swing in front and behind you in a pendulum-type action. This will give you a good idea of the type of backlift you need.

ON THE DEFENCE

Bat and pad, bat and pad, bat and pad. After you have played a defensive shot ask yourself whether there was any room between bat and pad. If the answer was 'yes' give yourself a kick in the pants. Anyone who is bowled through the gate, as it is called in cricket, has been made to look silly.

The advantages of bat and pad should be self-evident as you cannot be out lbw if the ball has first tickled your bat.

The forward defensive stroke must not become a tired lean into the ball. The left leg must come forward and the bat should arrive just after it. Naturally the body will follow the leg forward and at the moment of impact the bat must be angled at about 60 degrees from the ground. One of the best tests of the effectiveness of a forward defensive stroke is the positioning of the head, which must be watching the ball on to the bat. If the head is thrown back the whole stroke is wrong.

The back defensive stroke must be the easiest in cricket. A short step backwards, putting the weight on to the back foot, head over the ball and looking down, and the left elbow round about nose height to help keep the bat straight. If you find you are popping the ball perilously close to silly mid-off, it is advisable to have a look at your right hand. The stroke is essentially left-handed because the left hand naturally angles the bat. When the bottom hand does anything more than rest on the bat, the angle will be wrong and the ball will be liable to go in the air.

I cannot tell the individual player that a good-length ball pitches 'x' feet in front of him and a short ball 'y' feet. It is the Greig and Pilling question all over again. It depends how tall you are.

Similarly it is foolish to be dogmatic about whether to go forward or backwards as a matter of policy at the start of innings. Time was when nearly every coach told his charges to go forward as a matter of course. It never was cast-iron advice and I certainly don't regard it as such today.

My answer to the 'forward or back?' question is 'it depends on the state of the wicket'. I rarely go in higher than number six these days. Even at the rate England and Leicestershire have sometimes collapsed over the past few years, I have still had enough time to study the bowling from the pavilion.

If the ball is seaming a bit I would always tend to go forward to a bowler of Tom Cartwright's calibre. He would be likely to move one into me and if I am on the back foot I would have no chance of escaping an lbw decision.

If the ball is lifting from on or about a length, I would tend to go back. Go forward in a case like this and you are likely to get the ball on the glove or bat handle, or even in the mouth.

Different players have different inclinations, as a look at the recent England regulars will show. John Edrich (Surrey) is essentially a back-foot player, while Brian Luckhurst (Kent) is a front-foot player. Geoff Boycott (Yorkshire) has a preference for the back foot, but like all class batsmen, he is ready to change if the conditions dictate. He goes in first, of course, and therefore must build up his own dossier of what is happening from the first ball—he cannot spend a couple of hours assessing the situation from the balcony.

DRIVING

I like driving off the front foot and I like to see other batsmen do the same. The drive is a good shot to watch, a sign that a batsman is in the groove and playing attacking cricket.

The best drivers of the ball of my generation have fitted into two categories. There has been a savage breed, led by Ted Dexter and Peter May, who have excited crowds with the power and fluency of their shots. Then there has been the timers of the ball, led by Len Hutton and Colin Cowdrey, whose strokes were delicate and effortless. All four of these— each an England captain—hit the ball beautifully in front of the wicket.

If I have a slight preference for the touch players, it is probably because I have always regarded my boyhood idol, Len Hutton, as the greatest of them all. I remember that when I scored a hundred for Yorkshire early in my career J. M. Kilburn of the *Yorkshire Post* wrote that my cover driving was comparable to that of Wally Hammond or Len Hutton at their best. Praise indeed! I wish I could drive like that all the time.

It is the willow of your bat which drives the ball to the boundary although one could argue that the two vital factors in driving are not the bat at all but the body and the feet. Driving is comparable to throwing a punch at boxing where the positioning of the body and the feet do the damage, and the fist is merely their instrument.

Coaches usually emphasise the necessity of getting the feet to the pitch of the ball when driving; while this is true enough I would rather there was a joint emphasis on feet *and* body. There is no point in pushing the left leg forward if the body does not follow it; if you do this you will get no power in the stroke and, what is worse, you will be liable to pop the ball in the air.

In many ways the drive is a development of the forward defensive stroke—in each case it is vital to get one's body to the pitch of the ball and to get one's head over the top of it. Also, you must not show the bowler any gate.

Get to the pitch of the ball, strike the ball when it is parallel to the left foot, follow through with a triumphant arc and resist the temptation to look up too soon. As part of the follow-through the body will pivot at the hips and your torso will swing round so that you are facing the direction in which you have hit the ball.

Backlift and the role of the bottom hand are two elements of driving about which I find it hard to be dogmatic. Technically you need generous backlift, and the left hand should guide the stroke although the right plays a positive role by giving the stroke power.

Yet one of the most attractive front-foot players in

England in recent years has been Basil D'Oliveira and he has very little backlift, probably because he was brought up on bad South African wickets; if he lifted the bat high, the ball was liable to creep through.

There is sometimes a touch of 'kidology' about D'Oliveira's play. He will play back to encourage the bowler to pitch up, then come forward and crack the ball. In all these questions of forward or back, front foot or back foot, you have to remember the bowler's psychology.

To compensate for this lack of backlift, D'Oliveira has remarkably strong forearms.

His Worcester colleague, Jim Yardley, has very little backlift either. Nor has Ajit Wadekar, the Indian captain, nor Ken Suttle (Sussex). Yet Suttle scored more than 30,000 runs in first-class cricket. You can get along without backlift although no one should try to do so as a conscious change of style.

Equally, some players disregard the textbook and allow the right hand to dominate the direction of their shots. This is known as 'bottom handing' and to say that a player 'bottom hands the ball away' is regarded in some circles as akin to accusing him of eating three lots of tea.

As always there are famous exceptions. Douglas Insole, a former England batsman and later chairman of the selectors, was the most notorious in my memory. He bottom-handed so blatantly that he was liable to give any self-respecting coach apoplexy. Two later England batsmen, John Edrich and Brian Luckhurst, also used the bottom hand, although not nearly to the same extent.

You could say that these players are exceptions which prove the rule. I'm not keen in proving and disproving rules in cricket: the game is not a rigid intellectual exercise. I would prefer to say that although there is a natural and majority way of doing things on the field—there is, thankfully, room for the talented chap who goes against the mainstream of theory.

I hope, incidentally, that I don't have to tell anyone that

balls on the off-side should be driven on the off-side and so on. If you have other ideas I suggest you try lawn tennis as a summer sport. But there is one point about the direction of drives which young batsmen ought to note: Don't be too clever when trying to pierce the field. I know it is frustrating to hit your on-drive sweetly in the middle of the bat and then find it travels so quickly to wide mid-on that you don't even get a single. The temptation to place your next drive ought to be resisted. Don't get too ambitious unless things are definitely going your way. Placing your drives a couple of yards one way and then the other is a highly difficult business which is often too much for first-class players.

You can, of course, drive off the back foot. The shot is an extension of the backward defensive stroke but to attack you must have backlift (no question about it this time!) otherwise the ball will not go very far. You need powerful wrists and forearms, too, and I think 90 per cent of schoolboys will not be strong enough to score many runs this way.

Finally, there is the square drive. And lest there should be any confusion between the square cut, which I will mention in a moment, and the square drive, remember that the drive is the front-foot shot and the cut should always be played off the back foot.

The square drive is played to a ball short of the half-volley and probably outside the line of off-stump. It is a shot to play when you are going well, angling your bat towards the covers. It is profitable because there is rarely a man square of the wicket on the off-side and you often see it played on Sundays by batsmen who would hardly consider it during the week.

I like the square drive because it scores runs. A good cover drive can earn nothing but a round of applause. A good square drive rarely fails to produce runs. But there is an element of risk.

THE CUT

The cut, of course, was that so-and-so shot which Arthur Mitchell told me to leave at Farsley. In one sense he was right —the cut is a bold, full-blooded shot which ought to be played with a bit of arrogance. In the nets at Headingley I probably played the shot with the timidity of a raw 14-year-old. This is not the way.

The cut, square or late, is a back-foot shot. It is played to a short ball *outside* the off stump, although foolhardy types occasionally cut balls on their stumps. By all means make room for yourself by stepping to leg—some batsmen might even step outside the leg stump—but do not cut unless the ball is outside off. You are cutting the ball because it is outside the off, and because a horizontal bat is the best way to reach it; if it was short and on your stumps you would not cut.

When cutting you will angle your bat downwards slightly to keep the ball down. Also you are playing across the line. It's worth thinking about the odds, isn't it? I love cutting but I would think twice about doing so if I had just come in and the score was 52 for four. Batting is a bit like poker—you have to keep on weighing the risks against the likely rewards.

It may seem as though the slow bowler is the man to cut as he gives you time to get into position for what is not an easy stroke. But I wonder. The one thing you want when cutting is evenness of bounce. If you try to cut a spinning ball, you may find you have picked one which stands up a little.

By all means cut, and may all your edges be bottom and not top. When you cut square, hit the ball as though you're trying to break it in two. Don't pretty-pretty about.

I've already given you enough clues as to the way I think the shot ought to be played and here it is in capsule: back foot across and the weight on it, bat withdrawn to the shoulder and then brought powerfully to strike the ball, plenty of wrist in the shot, and the head firm throughout the shot.

Often young batsmen play what I would call a half-cut. They

put their front foot down the wicket, realise they have mis-judged the length of the ball, and wave their bats in a half-hearted fashion. Don't do this.

The late cut is a delightful shot to play. All crowds love it and it will raise a universal chuckle or perhaps even a cheer. Unfortunately it is as difficult as it is delightful although one of its compensations is that if you do not connect properly you are likely to miss the ball altogether and not get a snick.

Essentially the shot is a question of re-directing the ball . . . for some reason you have not hit it so far and suddenly it is square of the wicket, or even a shade behind it, and nicely within range of the bottom half of your bat. You reach out, with your weight on the back foot, and tickle the ball down-wards and away from slip. Usually it is all so, so gentle, be-cause the stroke is razor fine. Sometimes you may give the ball a definite nudge—this will depend upon your stance, timing and the position of the field.

Denis Compton, who managed to cock a snook at most rules in the book, used to play a second-thought cut. He would go down the wicket, the bowler would see him coming and drop the ball short, and Compton would have to fish behind him with his feet all over the place. It happens to most of us some time. But you have to be good to mount a rescue oper-ation as effectively as Compton.

PULL, HOOK AND SWEEP

Cut a ball which is short and outside your off-stump, pull a ball which is short and on your midriff and—perhaps—hook a ball which is very short and on your nose.

The term 'pull' covers a wide range of shots. It includes horizontal swings of the bat which send the ball anywhere in an arc from wide mid-on to fine leg.

The pull is not too readily definable a stroke. The purists might argue that it is not much of a shot, but I believe it takes skill to play it consistently against quality bowling. You have got to be quick, both in spotting the ball which is a shade short and in positioning your feet so that you have room to swing. Remember that the pull is essentially a back-foot shot. There is something wrong if you are leaning forward to a short ball and playing across the line.

Remember, too, that you must keep the ball down. There is no point swinging willy-nilly and sending the ball in the air. I played a lot of pull shots in Australia in 1970–1 and they proved profitable; they wouldn't have been if I had become careless about the angle of my bat.

The hook is at once both the most spectacular and the most dangerous shot in cricket. The quick bowler sends down a bouncer, the batsman swings, there is a clean crack, and the ball whistles over square leg for six . . . Every young batsman dreams about moments like these. I know I did.

Forget your dreams, forget the hook. Play it in your benefit match when you're 115 not out. Play it when you're feeling tired after completing your hundredth hundred. Play it at the Scarborough festival.

I'm sorry if I sound like an old fogey. The fact is that the hook is a difficult and perhaps dangerous shot for schoolboys to play. What is more, to play the shot with any regularity you have to be looking for it—you have to expect a contest between yourself and a 'quickie' who is going to throw in a few short ones to try to shake you. Such a contest took place between Keith Stackpole and John Snow in Australia but it is not likely in schools matches.

The hook is a beautiful shot. Gary Sobers, who can do everything in cricket, plays it so easily and smoothly. I remember Colin Cowdrey's hooking against Wes Hall in the West Indies in 1959–60. It was sharp and courageous—one of the most exciting sights I have seen on a cricket field.

Colin hooked in that season because he had to. He is not a hooker by conviction, as it were, although he is good enough to play the stroke when the chances come along.

The hooking addict always gives the bowler too much of a

chance of getting him out. Clive Lloyd (Lancashire and West Indies) couldn't leave the hook alone when he toured England in 1969. He kept getting himself out. Cyril Washbrook, Hutton's opening partner for England, was another who nibbled too often.

Bill Edrich, who often went in number three below Hutton and Washbrook, had the unhappy habit of hooking down deep square leg's throat.

The sweep provokes almost as much delight as the late cut because it is a shot which looks cheeky and which can throw the bowler and fieldsmen off their stride. I regard it with a certain amount of suspicion. It can be played only to a certain type of ball and there is a danger that a boy will be so 'chuffed' if he sweeps once that he will try to play the shot too often and get himself out.

The ball to sweep has to be slow and preferably just outside the line of leg stump. If the ball is well outside the leg stump you will be able to swing it happily when it arrives. You can also sweep from outside the off stump but you must make sure your front leg is outside the off, so that if you miss the ball it will hit your leg. Sweeping from outside off is particularly effective against the off-spinner on a turning wicket.

The sweep is what it says it is. You go down on the right knee and run the bat round daisy-high in a circular motion in front of you. The bat may start well on the off-side and sweep through more than 90 degrees, or the sweep may be very wristy and the bat travel only through a small segment. Your head must be over the ball and, as a result, the top of your left pad will be brushing up into your left armpit. If you miss the ball it will probably hit you on the left pad but there should be little fear of an lbw decision because you will be well down the wicket and either outside leg stump or very near it, or outside off. This is one shot where the right (or bottom) hand *can* take control, hitting with a downward movement as you sweep to ensure that you keep the ball on the floor.

The length of the ball is one factor I have not mentioned yet and it is an important one. Technically the ball you are most likely to sweep will be one of good length because you are well forward to play the shot with your bat stretching in front of you. In practice you are more likely to sweep the overpitched ball . . . your knee will drop down, you won't reach forward but rather play a slightly cramped shot which catches the ball on the volley. It takes a quality batsman to sweep the good-length ball; the novice will often sweep when he ought to be on-driving.

Kenny Barrington used to sweep so hard that the sound of the bat hitting the ball sounded like a rifle shot. Colin Cowdrey's sweep is much more delicate. He plays the shot with an almost vertical bat instead of a cross-bat. This travels in an arc from mid-off to fine leg, which is where the ball finishes up.

Geoff Boycott is a late convert to the sweep, and he gives the shot plenty of follow-through, as it were. At the risk of being a bore, it is worth pointing out that Boycott was skilful enough to play the sweep for years before it became a regular feature of his play. But until recently he did not consider that the return was worth the risk.

TAKING GUARD

Many youngsters take middle stump if the bowling looks unpleasantly quick, middle-and-leg if they are facing seamers, and leg stump if they fancy their chances against some erratic spinner. Really life is not that simple.

My normal guard is middle-and-leg, and so is that of the majority of first-class players irrespective of the pace of the bowling. But I am always ready to vary my guard if the conditions dictate.

On a wicket where the off-spinner is doing a fair amount— perhaps turning the ball from outside off to outside leg—I have seen Colin Cowdrey, Barry Richards and a fair few others take guard two to three inches outside leg stump. I've done the same myself. The aim, naturally enough, is to give

Four more bowling grips: above, the inswinger (left) and the outswinger, with
the seam slanted and pointing towards the slips; the difference in grip is slight and
the main difference is in the bowling delivery. Below, left, the leg-break grip,
with the spin coming from the wrist and the two fingers tucked under the ball;
below right, a front view of the googly.

The start of the forward defensive stroke, above left, with the front leg established and bending into the shot, and the left arm controlling the bat; right, the finish of the stroke: the left leg is bent into the shot with the knee over the toe, the left arm is well up to ensure control and the bat handle is well forward. My head is over the ball, and my bat and pad are together.
Getting into position for the backward defensive stroke I have moved my right leg back and slightly across. Bottom right, the finish of the shot: my left hand is controlling the bat and only the thumb and first finger of my right hand are touching the handle.

oneself plenty of room for manœuvre as the ball comes in from the off.

Incidentally, as you ask for 'two' for middle-and-leg and 'one' for leg stump, it doesn't follow that you ask for 'minus one' if you want a guard outside leg stump! Ask for leg stump, then move outside it.

I often take leg stump when a slow left-armer is bowling over the wicket into rough outside my leg stump and trying to get one to come back and bowl me round my legs. I can remember doing it against Don Wilson soon after I left Yorkshire and it is an effective tactic.

Occasionally I will take a guard of middle stump, as I did when I found myself on a nasty track at Bristol. The ball was turning from the off and keeping low at the same time. It was a nasty combination but a guard of middle—which cuts down your gate—plus a resolve to play off the front foot, earned me some runs. I would also take middle if a seamer was making the ball come in a little and keep low.

Would I ever take a guard further across than middle? Perhaps even off stump? I have never asked for either of these guards but I expect I have been further across than middle at the moment of delivery when a left-armer has been bowling over the wicket and has been angling the ball towards rough outside my off stump. But the further across you go, the more vulnerable your leg stump becomes. If in doubt, I would always err towards the leg. Although a discussion about guards may seem academic for young players, they would be foolish to take middle-and-leg unthinkingly. That extra bit of insight usually pays dividends.

BUILDING AN INNINGS

Where, oh where, are all the up-and-coming England batsmen? Buried under a mountain of Gillette razor blades and John Player's cigarettes, is my reply.

Sadly it is not now possible for middle-order batsmen to build an innings in the way they used to. The openers are fortunate in that they can play themselves in a little, even in 40-over Sunday cricket. But when the middle order come in, they find they have to score runs straightaway. One of the results can be seen in the performance of the England middle order from the moment when one-day cricket became a force in our game—we have collapsed time and again. Equally worrying is that the young middle-order men are not coming through; all we have is openers.

I hope I don't sound too much like an old reactionary. I hope, too, that no one will dub me as being against one-day cricket because I am not. I do think, though, that the one-day game should merely be the icing on top of the three-day cake.

For similar reasons I hope coaches and schoolmasters will not encourage limited-over games because if they do their charges may never have the chance to build an innings from one season to the next.

I am *not* advocating that young players should be encouraged to go to the wicket, spend three-quarters of an hour scratching around and then play their first aggressive shot. If the first ball you receive is a long hop, belt it with all your might and be thankful.

But more than likely you will have to wait for your long hop. The sight of you, a new batsman, will encourage the bowlers and the captain will try to hustle and unsettle you. The first half-hour of a first-class innings is the vital time; in one-day minor cricket this time might be scaled down to twenty minutes but the principle is the same.

Keep bat and pad together, have a good look at the bowling, attune yourself to the pace of the wicket and don't play any risky shots. . . . All this is sound advice at the start of an innings. I know the longer there is a nought against your name the worse it is, but for goodness' sake don't start fencing outside the off stump and try to nudge a cheap run. Play yourself in and soon you will feel the ball making a rich sound on your bat. That is the time to start increasing the pace.

All this applies in normal circumstances and to a batsman who can reasonably expect to score runs. It hardly applies to the shut-eyes-and-hope player who is going in as high as number eleven only because there isn't a number twelve. His tactics are determined by the state of the game as, indeed, are those of everyone else. A middle-order batsman doesn't take a good sounding of the conditions when his side needs twenty runs in ten minutes.

RUNNING BETWEEN THE WICKETS

Denis Compton must be the only man to have run out his brother in his benefit match! Compton, talented in so many ways, was an appalling judge of a run. Whenever he called, the batsman at the other end regarded it as only the opening of negotiations. Bill Edrich, who batted with him for Middlesex and England, used to say his usual call was: 'Yes! *No!!* Sorry . . .'

Geoff Boycott is another bad caller. Odd that a batsman who has mastered every other art of batting and who can rank among the great players should be unable to do a simple thing like judge a run. It is easy to make jokes about Compton's and Boycott's failing but really it is not funny. A run out is a wicket thrown away. It is a shocking waste. It can harm a team's morale although it should not do so.

Excuse my saying so, but I am an excellent judge of a run. Although it's tempting fate I am happy to say that I am very rarely involved in a run out. One way to avoid a run out is to stay awake at the non-striking end: self-evident but true. Another is to run for the pair of you and not for yourself. One sure method of asking for trouble is to look for a run because you yourself want to get away from a nasty bowler or steal the strike next over.

There are only three calls: yes, no, and wait. The striker calls if the ball goes in front of the wicket or square of it, the non-striker if it goes behind. Trust your partner: if you feel you need to look round for the ball before responding to his call, you ought to put your heads together in practice and work something out.

I said there are three calls but in fact there are four. The fourth is to say nothing and, in a curious way, it is the most effective of the lot. It shows that two cricketing brains are working in harmony and reacting automatically to a situation. It takes time, of course, for an understanding like this to develop. Almost certainly, young players are best advised to stick to the three basic calls.

Steal a quick single if you can. It rattles the bowling side and frustrates the bowler; it is a sign of the batsman's confidence and eagerness to dominate. Bobby Simpson, the former Australia captain, was a wonderful judge of a quick run. You would keep thinking you had him but he would get home by six inches.

The fastest runner in county cricket today is Asif Iqbal (Kent) who can run one and a half to most batsmen's one. Clive Lloyd (Lancashire) is only a couple of yards behind him. The Kent pair of Mike Denness and Brian Luckhurst are an excellent model for all youngsters.

SOME OUTSTANDING BATSMEN

One batsman I've not mentioned yet, but one who could become even more of a force on the world scene is *Ian Chappell*, who succeeded Bill Lawry as captain of Australia.

Chappell is an oddity in that he seems to be better equipped for English conditions than he does for those in Australia. He is very quick on his feet, something which one rarely sees these days despite the emphasis which coaches rightly put on footwork. He is so quick that it is not easy to bowl at him.

I remember Derek Underwood and myself bowling at Chappell in a Test at Headingley in 1968. The wicket was 'going' a bit and but for Chappell's footwork we could well have got on top.

He is well built for quick movement against slow bowling, being lithe and under six foot. Yet curiously against the quicker bowling on his home pitches he becomes leaden-footed and gets himself into trouble.

The reason is that he is too keen to get behind the line of the ball. He gets his back foot right across and is caught square on to the bowler with his feet wide apart and anchoring him. He puts himself in the ideal position to be caught by the ball rising off a length on the hard Australian pitches—if he was a shade more sideways on, he would be much happier. As it was, John Snow parted his hair once or twice in Australia.

Chappell would do well to take one or two hints from a former Australian captain, Bobby Simpson, who was a great leaver-alone of fast bowling.

A lot of Chappell's runs come through mid-wicket; also, he is a good square-cutter. This might sound an odd combination of strengths until one studies his grip. In cricketing parlance he 'goes underneath a bit'. This is a form of bottom-handing. Chappell moves his bottom hand further round his bat handle, so that the palm of his hand faces upwards rather than facing the bowler. If you try doing this, you'll find your bottom hand will drag your shots across to the on-side. It will also give you extra power and control when you try cuts and chopping-type movements square of the wicket on the off. Hence Chappell's apparently diverse strengths. On the reverse side, this unusual grip limits him off the front foot on the off-side.

Chappell is a chirpy character . . . and not only in contrast to Bill Lawry, his predecessor, who could be a dour Aussie. He has the makings of a good captain. He's a good first slip and he's learnt to read spin bowling from that position. He is a leg-break bowler who is worth bowling in Tests. Yet there is that one doubt against pace bowling.

Geoff Boycott, the most consistent scorer of runs in the world today, used to struggle just outside the off stump and tended to fish for the ball which was moving away from him. Grahame Corling, a good but not outstanding Test bowler for Australia, had him more than once this way.

I feel that Boycott is still a little vulnerable to this type of ball. But the delivery has to be spot on. If it is six inches short he will be on the back foot, clipping it away with that crouching action of his; if it is six inches wide, the bowler has equally no chance because Boycott knows where his off stump is to within a coat of paint.

His bat-and-pad technique can make bowling at him a miserable affair. As an off-spinner I would never expect to bowl him through the gate, nor would I expect his bat to be so far forward on its own to enable a tickle to flick through to a backward short leg. Any close catch is likely to be one which pops after being jammed between bat and pad.

Having known Boycott over the years I've been able to see how he has asserted himself more and more. In the past two or three years it has become impossible to bowl half-volleys at him; previously he would have patted a good half of them down the wicket. Now he is powerful off the front foot.

The South Africans Mike Procter and Barry Richards are the only two I can think of who may be better; this is because they are physically stronger and because they have been brought up on better wickets.

I have one complaint about Boycott's batting and that is he fails to dominate as quickly as he might, especially in county cricket. Often he is at his best when he has passed his century. He has no need to wait so long. He is a great batsman—not a phrase I would use lightly—and much of the bowling he faces in county cricket is by no means great. He must show them his pedigree sooner.

Boycott still has this horror of getting out, which I like to see. He always used to go into his shell for two or three hours when he arrived back in the dressing room. Now the period of recovery has got a bit shorter!

Barry Richards used to be a complete contrast to Boycott in terms of attitude. He used to set off fairly fast, reach 50 or 60, and then throw his wicket away. He was impetuous: the century was there for the taking but Richards wasn't prepared to wait. On his good days he would get his hundred but even then he did not have the big innings mentality and got out too often in the 120s.

Then he started playing for a dollar a run in Australia. And the big scores came much more frequently!

As I have mentioned, Richards' history of playing on good wickets has given him tremendous confidence in driving off the front foot. I hope readers do not think I'm making excuses for our home-grown players because I'm not. Roy Marshall (Hampshire) is another example of an overseas player—in this case a West Indian—benefiting from good wickets. For years Marshall scored consistently faster than the great majority of English batsmen, at times incredibly so. He will tell you that the reason is that he was brought up to expect that ball to come on to the bat firm and true. Some of this rubs off on to England players when we tour abroad and we always come back from Australia or the West Indies feeling better batsmen.

But Richards, of course, is more than just a product of good wickets. He has masses of natural ability into the bargain. What's more he is good all round and it is not easy to find a flaw in his make-up.

One thing I have noticed as an off-spinner is that he likes to hit the ball coming into him square on the off-side. (Remember what I said about the square drive being profitable?) He does leave a gap which can be exploited if you can turn the ball into him. But at what cost! You can get every batsman out some time . . . the question is 'how many runs later?'

Richards is fast down the wicket, unusually so for a big man.

Sometimes I wonder whether he comes down by numbers: third and fifth of one over, second and fifth next, and so on. If this sounds unworthy of a world-class batsman, I can assure younger readers that sometimes this can be an effective way of throwing a bowler off his length. But you have to be as quick as Richards or Chappell to succeed. The bowler will vary his length if you do not wait until he is actually releasing the ball.

Finally, to the best player I have ever seen, *Gary Sobers*. It pains me a little to admit that there has been a better batsman than Len Hutton but it must be said.

There is only one type of wicket on which I would fancy my side's chances of getting rid of Sobers cheaply and that is the one with a bit of grass on top which was moving the ball off the seam. Sobers hits the ball on the up, unlike the vast majority of batsmen, and late deviation off the seam does give the fielding side just a chance.

I know Sobers does not get hatfuls of runs for Nottinghamshire, although he gets enough. There are reasons enough for this. He is head cook and bottle-washer and often he sacrifices his batting to concentrate on bowling and captaincy.

This, plus the fact that he has played too much cricket in the past three or four years, has meant that he has scored tens instead of fifties and fifties instead of hundreds. But is there any more beautiful batsman in the world when he is on song? I doubt it.

He has that pace of movement which sometimes comes easy to coloured athletes but not so often to white ones. It shows in the relaxed way he plays fast bowling—he is never ugly or hurried. He is perhaps the only batsman who has the timing to hit a bowler of John Snow's quality back over his head. His timing of shots, against the slow bowlers as well as the quickies, is even more remarkable when you think that he doesn't come down the wicket a lot. To a great extent he is a crease-bound player, and he has the eye, ball sense and reflexes to get away with it.

Sobers' bat always travels through a straight arc from wicket to wicket. Very rarely does it move horizontally. That is why he can often get a thick outside edge and escape. Because he plays so straight, the ball will ricochet off the edge and into the covers where the fieldsmen will be lucky to get a hand. If he played with an angled bat or a horizontal one, the ball would fly upwards for a catch.

I can understand Sobers not taking the brunt of the batting in three-day matches for Nottinghamshire but I do think he ought to go in higher than five or six in one-day matches. On Sundays there is no particular reason why he should not open; if he stays there for most of the 40 overs, as he is quite capable of doing, the other side will have a lot to do to win.

It all goes back to this question of the batsman setting out to dominate, which is a good note on which to end this chapter. Cricket is a batsman's game—at least so far as the dice is loaded, it is against the bowler.

Remember that when you walk to the wicket. The initiative is yours. Seize it as soon as you can.

3
Fast Bowling

Ask the majority of young bowlers what they bowl and they are likely to say 'medium pace' or 'seamers'. This is very true of club cricketers. They have not the rhythm or physique to bowl fast, and they haven't the guile to bowl slow; therefore they settle for a meaningless in-between.

Don't do this. I am not saying that no youngster should be a medium-pace bowler, far from it. But no one learning the game should become a trundler. If you are a medium-pacer aim to do something positive with every ball. Practise the in-swinger, practise the outswinger, and always be prepared to try something new.

I began life as a seam bowler and switched to off-spin by chance. I was playing in a schools match and bowling my seamers when I sent down a slower one which turned sharply.

'Don't waste your time bowling seam if you can turn off-breaks like that,' said the master who was umpiring for the opposition.

I didn't take him seriously and I was sixteen before I bowled an off-break in a match. I was playing in a Bradford League match at Saltaire and my team, Farsley, were in trouble. We had been bowled out for 58 on a wet track and they were 30 for one. Jack Firth, the Yorkshire and Leicestershire wicket-keeper, and the Farsley captain, tossed me the ball and said: 'Why don't you bowl some spinners?'

I did, and took five wickets for five. It occurred to me then that bowling off-spin was a good idea!

I would advise every young cricketer not to be so set in his ways that he cannot change his style or even his basic function in a side.

John Snow is a prize example of this. When he first went to Sussex as a teenager he was a batsman. Then he went away for a year and reappeared as a fast bowler. He had made the change because the club cricket in which he played was top heavy with batsmen; he disliked being a wallflower, and—as ever—there was plenty of room for a class fast bowler.

Years later, after he had just come into the England side, Snow found that he was bowling very much front on. He spent two winters coaching in South Africa and during that time he modified his action so that it was more side on. The result was more speed and a regular England place.

Alan Ward, although always a fast bowler, had to make a similar basic adjustment to his action. He was leaning forward as he ran up to the wicket, whipping his torso back just before delivery, then whipping it forward again for delivery. His body was moving back through more than ninety degrees and coming forward again. Not surprisingly he was warned that the pressure on his spine was dangerous.

He had to spend a winter sorting himself out. At the end of it he was a better bowler—an England bowler, in fact.

I had better steer off fast bowlers otherwise there'll be nothing left when I come to the main theme of the chapter! However there are a couple more prize examples of players who have switched roles. Kenny Barrington went to Surrey as a leg-break bowler. And one of the best-known of today's players was pointed out to Les Ames, the Kent manager, at a swimming pool as 'a good little off-break bowler'. Ames is supposed to have looked at the lad and not been over-impressed—he didn't look as though he had the strength to propel a ball twenty yards. The lad's name was Alan Knott.

IMPORTANCE OF THE BOWLER

There is an old cricketing joke about Francis Drake being the last bowler to be given any sort of honour. This sums up a common attitude in bowlers. They often think they are the silly so-and-sos who sweat and strain to produce balls for the batsman to belt to the boundary.

Sometimes there may be truth in this. I remember being told in the past that such-and-such a county wicket was slow because the local gentry played club cricket there and they had to be given every chance to make their fifties.

Silly so-and-sos or not, bowlers win matches. Surrey won the county championship seven times in succession in the fifties because they had Jim Laker and Tony Lock taking wickets and not because Peter May and Kenny Barrington piled up the runs. Other counties have had prolific run-scorers and have not had a smell of the title.

Yorkshire were the dominant side of the sixties although for much of that time our batting was most unpredictable. We used to rely on someone coming up trumps with the runs. It was our attack that made us such a good side. Fred Trueman was the spearhead, well supported by Tony Nicholson or Mel Ryan. I was the off-spinner, with Brian Close often weighing in with off-breaks and seamers. Don Wilson was the slow left-armer.

The strength of that attack was not only in its individuals but also in its balance. We had something for every type of wicket with Jack Hampshire in reserve as a leg-spinner. The Surrey attack which won the championship in 1971 is similarly balanced although they preferred the leg-spin of Intikhab Alam to the slow left-arm of Chris Waller.

It's sometimes said that Bill O'Reilly, the Australian leg-break bowler of the thirties, was the most dangerous bowler ever to walk on to a cricket field. That statement is one for the cricket historians to argue about, not me.

I know that if I had to choose one bowler of my generation to have in my side the names of Trueman and Lindwall would leap into my mind first.

The common image of a fast bowler is of a man of about 5 ft 9 in, almost as wide as he is tall, with a prominent backside and who down pints of beer with astonishing regularity. He swears at anyone who drops a catch and is generally surly and bad-tempered.

It does not matter what a fast bowler's dimensions are as long as he is strong. I suspect the image of the fast bowler being built like a Rugby League player is popular because men of this build—not over-tall and sturdy—are tough characters. And fast bowlers have to be tough.

Chris Old (Yorkshire) was unlucky not to go to Australia in 1970-1 and one main reason was that he had an unhappy history of injury. Alan Ward has been similarly plagued. Jeff Jones (Glamorgan) looked as good as any fast bowler in the world and was just starting to reach his peak when an elbow injury ended his career.

Some are lucky, some are unlucky . . . and some are just plain careless. An up-and-coming fast bowler should regard himself as an athlete just as much as the man who wants to run the hundred yards in ten seconds flat. He should take expert advice on his training and even his diet.

The most annoying injuries can be the little ones—the odd pull and strain which niggles you for weeks and weeks. Often these can be avoided.

In Australia, Ken Shuttleworth strained a leg muscle in an up-country match because he did not perform any warming-up exercises after a long coach ride.

I realise it can be infuriating for the fast bowler to sweat and strain while a batsman can be unathletic and bone idle yet still score runs. Cricket allows this double standard of fitness and the fast bowler will just have to accept it.

Many boys try to bowl ridiculously fast. You can see them running hell for leather up to the wicket, losing their rhythm when they arrive and then delivering a ball from the shoulder which makes nonsense of their run-up.

Some good fast bowlers come from this haphazard approach. Some, but not many. For every boy who becomes a fast bowler, nine out of ten resort to trundling or tweaking. Nevertheless I believe youngsters should have a go at fast bowling, even if they give up within half an hour, because it is an illogical art and no one knows in advance who can bowl fast and who cannot.

Only a very few are sufficiently gifted to make outstanding Test-match fast bowlers and I suppose England is doing well if she produces one every five years. Everyone could look at great fast bowlers like Trueman or Statham and admire their co-ordination, rhythm and physique. But you couldn't say why they had what they had. Of all the jobs a coach has to do, the one I would like least is that of trying to produce a world-class fast bowler. If he hasn't got it, you can't put it there.

RUN-UP

There is little relation between the length of a bowler's run-up and his speed, and if a young quickie feels that he is lacking speed usually the last thing he wants to do is increase his run-up.

Run-ups tend to be as illogical as fast bowling itself. Frank Tyson, who destroyed the Aussies in 1954–5, suddenly bounded forward with an extra powerful stride midway through his run.

John Price (Middlesex and England) is even more odd. His run must be a good 25 yards and he travels round a dog leg. From the pavilion end at Lord's he runs as though he is going to end up in the Taverners' Bar; then he suddenly straightens up after eight or nine yards. 'Pacing our Pythagoras' was one critic's recent description and certainly Price almost runs round two sides of a right-angled triangle. Yet the last strides of his run-up are strong and smooth, an ideal action. There is no explanation for the first, eccentric part of his run, but one cannot have the second part without the first.

Price is in his thirties and his habits are ingrained. If he was 14 it would be a different matter. If I was coach to a 14-year-old with a run like his I would certainly try to make him modify the first side of the triangle because it wastes time and it wastes energy.

The aim of the run-up is to enable the bowler to arrive at the wicket at speed and with momentum. But he must also be sufficiently well balanced so that he can discharge his power in the best possible way.

He will arrive at the wicket in a sideways-on position and (always assuming that we are talking about the right-hander) his left arm and left leg will be thrust forward just before the moment of delivery. The left-arm action has been important to nearly all the great bowlers because it gives them balance and especially direction at the vital time. I would advise a young bowler to make a bit of a show of his left-arm movement, perhaps putting his arm up there in a slightly exaggerated fashion. That way the left arm will not be easily forgotten.

It's probable that a fast bowler would lose his balance if he did not use his left arm, and certainly his delivery would come from a curious crouching action. Therefore he has to use the left arm.

In a slower action the use of the left arm is unlikely to be so much of a natural reflex action, but the left hand must be remembered or the slower bowler will be in danger of losing height.

Arriving in the position of having the left arm and left leg forward is only half the battle. The build-up is ineffective without a proper follow-through. At the moment of delivery the body pivots sharply on the front leg which will be taut and ready for the sudden strain. This means the body is brought into the action and it is from here that the pace of the ball comes. If you cannot appreciate how important the role of the body is, try bowling without the body-pivot or pivot only halfheartedly. You will straightaway find that you lose an alarming amount of power and control!

I believe there are two clues to the effectiveness of a bowler's run-up. One, and this applies to everything else in cricket, is the ease with which it is accomplished. The other is the movement of the head. Something is wrong if the head is rolling from side to side. It could be that the bowler's strides are too long and that he will have to rethink his run all over again.

In addition, the young fast bowler should pay attention to detail. I can remember Brian Statham complaining that many promising bowlers spoiled their rhythm by tossing their marker carelessly on the ground after they had measured their run-ups. Statham was meticulously in placing his marker at just the right spot and in treading to within an inch of it.

I can see his point. The odd inch twenty yards away from the wicket can mean the difference between a no-ball—which is effort wasted—and a thumping good delivery. Why put the whole operation at risk before you start?

No one likes fast bowling: it is just that some batsmen play it better than others. All fast bowling would, generally speaking, be tolerable if it was just straight up and down. It isn't . . . because the good quick bowler has the art of moving the ball off the seam and through the air.

SWING AND SEAM

The term 'swing bowling' is often used to cover bowling of any pace above slow which moves off the wicket. But I would like to distinguish between swing bowling—using your arm action, your grip on the ball and the atmosphere to move the ball *at genuine pace*—and seam bowling—using your grip to move the ball at medium pace.

Swing bowling, as I use the phrase, is an art we have lost in England. Sometimes when the atmosphere is particularly heavy you will find genuine swing bowling in our cricket. But it is rare. This was brought home to me most forcibly when I

Three stages in the off-drive: initially, my head is down, my backlift is straight and my front foot is moving to the ball; at the moment of contact my bat is still straight and my head is still down; and, bottom left, my left elbow is well up to ensure a good follow-through, my head is still down, and I am well balanced on my front foot. Bottom right, the on-drive. The principles are the same, but the angle of the bat tells you that my right hand is doing most of the work.

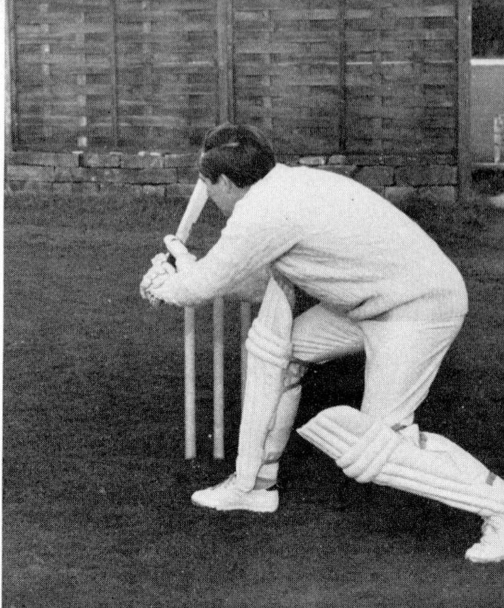

The late cut. The ball has pitched outside the off stump and I put my right leg back and across; right, the right foot is firmly established and the right hand is controlling the shot to ensure the bat's movement is downward; and below, I make contact. The fourth picture shows the difference between the late cut and the square cut: the basic action for the square cut is a downward chop.

faced Froggy Thomson, the wrong-footed Australian quick bowler, and thought at first that he was bowling boomerangs! He bowled me a ball which started outside off stump and swung so much that it missed leg. I estimated that almost all this swing was the result of his arm action, including a generous follow-through which sent the ball away from his body.

Thomson illustrates one of the frailties of swing bowling. It can be hard to control. Effective swing needs to be accurate and it needs to be late enough to catch the batsman by surprise. Also, of course, you cannot be too capricious if swing is your major weapon. An outswing bowler must have a field with a definite off-side bias and if he throws in a couple of inswingers an over he is going to prove expensive.

Ray Lindwall could swing the ball accurately, late and both ways, as I found out to my cost in the early fifties. Peter Loader, not as fast as Lindwall, could swing it as emphatically as anyone I ever saw. Fred Trueman developed a beautiful away-swinger which he used to more and more effect as he lost his pace. John Snow has also been working on an away-swinger which I expect we will see more and more often.

Although, as I've said, the most important element in swing is a slight adjustment of the angle of delivery, the away-swinger and in-swinger do require certain grips.

Perhaps 'grip' is the wrong word for the away-swinger because the ball is held quite loosely with the seam upright and pointing towards first slip. The first two fingers form a 'V', resting on either side of the seam, and the other three digits support the ball. When the arm comes over, it should definitely come across the body and the follow-through will take the right hand and arm to the left side of the body.

There is no point trying to bowl an away-swinger from wide of the crease because you are working against yourself. You must bowl from near the stumps and aim at or about the middle stump. If you are swinging the ball successfully you will be able to aim at middle-and-leg; if not, middle-and-off should be your target.

D

Fifteen years ago the inswinger was very popular in English cricket, probably because it was easy for a batsman to bowl from wide of the stumps, to give the ball a nudge inwards, and to have a galaxy of leg-side fieldsmen waiting for the batsman to try an adventurous shot. This method of bowling did nothing for cricket. It was 'slant' bowling rather than swing bowling, with the ball being pushed across the batsman's body at such an angle that it was difficult for him to attack.

In 1957 the law was changed. The number of on-side fieldsmen was limited to five, with only two of these being allowed behind the popping crease. This change was brought about by the quicker bowler and handicaps the slow bowler—a story which has been too familiar in my years of playing cricket.

Since then inswing bowling has become less popular: there is no longer any room for the slant artist although a genuine inswing bowler, as Alec Bedser was, will always find a place at the highest level.

I was going to say that the more height you can obtain with the inswinger, the better. Then I remembered that Bedser's action was by no means high—there is always someone who has his own entirely individual technique. Anyway Bedser, and all the good inswing bowlers I can remember, did thump down their left foot further to the off-side than they would have done normally. This puts them a shade squarer to the batsman.

The delivery action should be such that the right arm comes down on the right side of the body, another departure from the cricketing norm. A boy practising an inswing for the first time will do well to remember to bring his arm straight down. If he can manage this, plus the change in delivery stride, without falling forward on his face he is making progress.

As with the outswinger, grip the ball with the seam upright with the first finger running down the left of the seam and the second finger down the right. And, of course, angle the seam to fine leg and not to third man.

It's easy for me to sit back and say that this grip is right for this ball and so on. The grips are academically correct and no one will get very far by slanting the seam to gully and trying to bowl an inswinger. But I hope every learner will experiment within the broad frameworks I mention, because without experiment, cricket will become a feeble game.

4

Off-spin Bowling

I know I'm biased but for me there is no finer sight in cricket than a good slow bowler pitting his wits against a good batsman on a wicket which gives both of them a chance.

I have for long been optimistic about cricket's future. But the one big worry I have is that limited-over cricket will squeeze out the spinner. There is great temptation in 40-over and 60-over matches to play seamers and tell thcm to bowl outside the off stump. It is a temptation which must be resisted —the more spinners the better.

No one who hopes to be a slow bowler should be in a hurry. No one should become disheartened if he is playing in a school team, getting only the occasional bowl and not making much progress when he does. A batsman or a fast bowler often gets good returns in top-level cricket when he is in his late teens or early twenties. Slow bowlers rarely do.

Geoff Cope of Yorkshire is in his middle twenties, yet still learning the off-spinner's trade . . . he promises to be a good one, too. He is a much better bowler than I was at his age. Chris Waller, the Surrey slow left-armer is 25, yet he has just come on the scene and it could be four or five years before he is near his best.

Although I first played for Yorkshire in 1951 I did not become the regular off-spinner until five years later. I had been in competition with Bob Appleyard, that fine off-break bowler, and with Brian Close. I was 25 when I graduated and had already bowled thousands of overs. It was a good job I did not become discouraged.

Young slow bowlers are likely to lack temperament rather than technique. There are days when a batsman will get hold of a spinner and belt him all round the ground. The spinner can do nothing about it. But the next time the spinner comes on to bowl he has still to bowl to a length and line, to vary his flight and to avoid pushing the ball through too quickly.

Before we have a look at slow bowling in more detail there is one bit of advice I would like to give any spinner who is hoping to make cricket his career. That is: don't be a complete rabbit with the bat. Anyone who has sufficient ball sense to be a good spinner shouldn't have his castle sent in all directions within an over or so.

Twenty years ago the division of labour in first-class cricket was stricter than it is now. There were fewer batsmen who could bowl seam and fewer seamers who could bat a bit. One-day cricket has changed that.

Often the slow bowler is in and out of the side; if he is likely to make 15 or so runs, this can mean the difference between his playing or wandering back and forward with the drinks.

I was lucky. At school I was good enough (and cheeky enough!) to open both batting and bowling. I have always had two strings to my bow and think I might have become an England batsman if I had concentrated on this part of the game. No aspiring bowler—fast or slow—should make a joke of his batting.

THE BASICS

I have already mentioned the elements of the run-up and these are the same whether you are bowling off sixteen paces or off six. But the slow bowler should be wary of taking too long a delivery stride. A shortish stride will gain height and it allows the bowler to bring his arm across his body without trouble. This, in turn, makes it easier to spin the ball.

In some ways the run-up can hold quite unnecessary dangers for the slow bowlers simply because they tend to ignore this aspect of their game. Even if you are bowling nice and slow you have got to have a run-up. I always thought David Allen, the Gloucestershire and England off-spinner, could have been a better bowler if he had had a longer run-up.

One of the weapons a slow bowler needs is variation of pace and this is not easy to acquire off a run of two or three paces. Also I have found that a longer run-up, even when the approach is as slow as mine, helps give the bowler rhythm.

No slow bowler should become careless about his run-up. Again I was lucky and when I was 16 and 17 my run-up was used on occasions as a model by my coaches.

Twenty years later I find that sometimes I am not getting my left shoulder round far enough and getting full pivot at the moment of delivery. And then I find I am not spinning the ball enough. So as a remedy I try a tactic which I can recommend to all off-spinners—I bowl round the wicket for a couple of overs and this forces me to get some bite into my body pivot.

If you want to be a spin bowler first learn to *spin* the ball. I know some coaches will disagree with this and some young players will protest that they have been taught to bowl line and length first.

I have no sympathy with the length-and-line argument. Teach a lad to bowl length and line and what happens when he tries to spin the ball as well? He is all over the shop. It's far better to spin the ball first, then to worry about where it's going to pitch.

Every genuine slow bowler must make that ball spin as it leaves his hand. I have rarely found an off-spinner who doesn't give the ball a fair tweak but sometimes I'm disappointed when I see slow left-armers. Hardly any of them spin the ball as much as they might. Perhaps it is because they have the natural advantage of turning the ball away from the right-handed bat and they feel this is a substitute for plenty of spin. I don't agree, and think my argument is backed up by the number of left-armers who don't cash in on helpful wickets in the way they might.

Very few lads have such small hands that they can't spin a cricket ball properly. Lance Gibbs (Warwickshire and West Indies) and David Allen are fortunate in having extra long fingers. Mine are broad and strong through years of bowling but they are not long. No one should offer the excuse that his hands 'aren't made for spinning'. Similarly, a spinner has an obvious advantage if he is round about six-foot because the extra height gives more chance of extracting bounce from the wicket . . . and bounce is even more important than turn.

Whatever the strength of the fingers, they are always liable to split or develop sores. There is very little one can do to prevent this. In fact, looking back to 1961 and finding that Yorkshire played 39 first-class matches, I'm surprised that I still have an index finger on my right hand!

I have always rubbed Vaseline into my fingers and this has kept them fairly free of sores. Fred Titmus, who has probably bowled more overs than anyone else playing first-class cricket, has never had the slightest trouble with his fingers. On the other hand Jack Birkenshaw and Brian Close, both of whom bowled off-spin with me at Yorkshire, have had trouble not with the index finger but with the middle one. The cause must be a slight difference in their grip.

However long and strong a slow bowler's fingers may be, his greatest asset is the little grey cells up top. The best advice anyone could give to a spinner is *think*. Whatever the state of the game, whatever your bowling return at any given moment, think.

'How can I do this fellow? What will he do if I toss one up? Can he spot my quicker one?' Questions like these should be going through the slow bowler's head all the time. If you have two basic deliveries and you use them in the ratio of four: two every over irrespective of what the batsman is doing, you are not going to get very far.

THE OFF-SPINNER

The off-spin grip and delivery are often compared to turning a door-knob from left to right and this gives a fair idea of the mechanics of the operation.

There are two basic grips for the off-break but in each case it is the index finger of the right hand which imparts the spin on to the ball. The off-break, of course, is always turning into the right-handed batsman and away from the left-handed batsman.

For the normal off-spin grip, place the index finger *either* down the side of the seam or across the seam. Spread the supporting fingers wide, as wide as you can, for the more taut your grip the more you are likely to spin the ball. The thumb and the little finger will fall into place naturally and support the ball.

If you release the ball with a clockwise twist of the wrist, you will find that it spins in that direction. It might not change direction on pitching, though. For a beginner to get turn of any size, he will need a worn ball which he can grip firmly and a surface which will grip at the spinning ball.

I usually hold the ball with my fingers up against the seam, as do the majority of off-spinners. The exception with me is when I am playing with a ball which feels small. Then I will hold it across the seam. All cricket balls for first-class matches are supposed to be the same size. They are not. When wrapping your fingers round a ball becomes second nature, you soon notice even the slightest difference in size.

The off-spinner's basic ball is a dangerous one when it is nipping through. It is not difficult to imagine the type of wicket which helps spin. If you try to spin a tennis ball off your polished front hall, you will find it difficult because the ball does not get enough purchase to turn very much. Try on a carpet which has a thick pile on top, and the ball is much more likely to change course.

By the same token the off-spinner receives little help from

a hard, plumb wicket. That is why English off-spinners are so rarely effective in Australia, the West Indies and other hot climates. And although there should be some bounce in this type of wicket, it will be even bounce and the off-spinner will not be bowling fast enough to exploit it.

When David Allen and I toured the West Indies in 1959–60 neither of us had much success in terms of figures. I took only four wickets at an average of 95 apiece and, as a result, was somewhat prematurely written off as a non-bowler on plumb wickets. I think the point the critics missed was that bowling is a team game and that David Allen and I were bowling as a unit.

Our spearhead was Fred Trueman and Brian Statham, who were most effective in bursts of three-quarters of an hour in the heat. Then the off-spinners had to come on and try to contain the batsmen while the quickies recovered their wind. We would probably have got the odd extra wicket—and perhaps better figures—if we had experimented more. But one loose over could so easily have lost us the initiative and meant that the quickies returned to face batsmen in full flow. Therefore we bowled within the team plan.

But back to the off-spinner, who is much more likely to be effective on the wicket which is crumbling after use, where the surface is breaking up and the ball can grip the surface. Every wicket will help the off-spinner . . . eventually. The question is whether he will get turn on the second day, the third day or a week next Tuesday.

Most English wickets will help the spinner in a three-day game. After the first few weeks of the summer, grounds like Lord's and the Oval, which are played on almost continuously, may have a spot which the spinners can exploit on the first day. On a good track at Trent Bridge, traditionally a batsman's wicket, Test bowlers may still be looking for signs of encouragement on the fourth day. Old Trafford used to be similar but recently it has taken spin on the third day.

The off-spinner, like all slow bowlers, should be thinking of

which end he wants to bowl from before his captain puts him
on. And choice of ends is not a technicality which should con-
cern only first-class players.

Often in schools or club cricket one of the wickets will be
worn and much more amenable to spin than the other. It is
even more likely that the square will slope one way or the
other.

Even if you are playing on a perfectly flat, true strip, there is
a chance that the wind will help the off-spinner at one end and
hinder him at the other.

Usually the off-spinner will want to bowl into a wind which
is blowing from left to right. Usually, but not always. It is a
mistake to think that the most successful off-spinner is necessarily the one who turns the ball the most.

A ball which turns three feet isn't likely to get anyone out
because it will end up outside the leg stump. A ball which turns
two or three inches but turns quickly is much more dangerous.

There may therefore be times when the off-spinner prefers to
bowl into a wind which puts a brake on his spin.

I always like to bowl from the pavilion end at Lord's because the ground slopes from the Mound Stand down towards
the Taverners' Bar and helps my off-break. Fred Titmus does
most of his bowling from that end, too, while the leg-spinner,
Harry Latchman, naturally prefers the Nursery End.

At Leicester the ground slopes with the wicket, not across it,
with the pavilion as the 'bottom end'. I always prefer to bowl
down the hill and this helps the ball run into the bat. At Bradford, or so the story goes, there is a slight ridge which helps
anyone bowling from the football ground end. I have always
preferred that end.

The good off-spinner will be studying the batsman and the
conditions before his captain calls on him. And if the wicket
looks a monstrous gift to the batsman, a little kidology might
not be out of place. Don't say in a loud voice: 'Nothing for
me in this, is there, skipper?' Try examining a spot in the
wicket which is going to help you—whether there is one or not.

Field placing is important. Most slow bowlers have a fair idea of the field they want but I think many make the mistake of muttering 'Cover, extra, mid-off . . .' and leaving it at that. Cover point can refer to a fair chunk of the field; so can any position outside the close-catching area.

Let us assume I am bowling right-handed off-spin to a batsman on a track which is giving me little help. I would have a leg-slip, four other men on the leg-side, and four on the off.

I have only one close catcher, the leg-slip. I choose him in preference to the slip so that the batsman doesn't feel free to flick the ball off his legs when I get it to come into him. Anyway, the wicketkeeper can always catch the thin outside edge.

I will be bowling on or about off-stump. The batsman should be able to stroke the ball into the covers without trouble. But unless I pitch on a bad length he shouldn't be able to hit me to the square off-side boundary. For this reason I have three men on the off-side saving one—one of them just behind the wicket to discourage the square drive, the other two in the covers.

The placing of these three is important. They should be just near enough to stop the batsman running a single, but no nearer because this gives them the maximum chance of stopping the cover drive. The other man on the off-side is at deep mid-off to prevent the straight hit if I toss one up or the batsman is tempted to come down the wicket at me.

The four men on the leg side are also there to save the one —provided I am bowling well and the batsman is quiet. If he was swinging me from the off-stump to behind square on the leg-side I would move my backward square leg deeper. Another acceptable defensive tactic is to move the man between mid-on and mid-wicket back to long on.

If the wicket is helping me and starting to turn I do not shake up my basic field too drastically unless I have runs to play with! I move my deep mid-off up to save the one and one of the cover fieldsmen goes to forward short leg. I can always crowd the batsman later on. And, indeed, I would be foolish not to as soon as the turn starts to bring results.

OFF-SPIN VARIATIONS

Right, you can bowl an off-break on line and length which turns . . . The next thing is to learn something different. One basic type of delivery is not going to get you very far.

For a start you must develop a quicker ball. It is not difficult and it is fun practising disguising it until the last minute.

More significantly, use the crease. Don't bowl every ball with your torso brushing the stumps because this means that the batsman always knows at what angle the ball is going to come at him.

Roy Tattersall, the former Lancashire and England off-spinner, used to vary his deliveries in a different way—by sometimes bowling a yard short of the crease and trying to fox the batsman that way, as did Peter Walker (Glamorgan). By all means try this although you'll probably end up thinking as I do, that the main result is to give the batsman an extra yard in which to see the ball.

The new lbw law, introduced at the start of the 1970 season, made off-spin bowling that much more problematical but fortunately we need not go into detail on this as the law was changed for the start of the 1972 season. Now, a batsman can be out if the ball pitches outside off-stump and hits the pad between wicket and wicket, provided the batsman is playing a shot. He can also be out if his leg is outside the off-stump and if he doesn't play a shot, providing the ball would have hit the wicket.

The idea of the law is plain. It is to make the batsman play with the bat and not the pad. Unfortunately it is open to misuse because it is easy to stick a pad down the wicket and wave the bat, thereby playing a mock stroke. It is easy for professional players, that is—I would strongly advise a young player not to chance his arm in this way.

Most off-spinners, including myself, Fred Titmus, Jack

Birkenshaw and John Mortimore, try to bowl a ball which swings from leg to off. This ball starts on leg stump and swings out a shade to the line of off-stump.

It is essential, too, to flight the occasional ball. The batsman is always looking for what he regards as an easy hit against the spinners and he may lose his head if he sees one go in the air. I aim my flighted ball so that it drops on normal length and often the batsman will not come forward to hit as he should. If I'm in luck he'll be striking the ball on the up from his crease and getting badly underneath it.

The quicker one is a useful ball at the death—the last ball of an over or a session. Bowl it as a yorker, aiming straight at the batsman's block hole. He will be looking to drive you and perhaps too ready to lift the bat. The yorker may well surprise him.

5
Leg Spin and Slow Left Arm

Leg-spinners are on the way back and everyone in cricket should be glad of it. In the mid-sixties you could go round the counties totting up the leg-spinners and still have fingers left on one hand.

Now we have Intikhab Alam (Surrey and Pakistan), Robin Hobbs (Essex) and Mushtaq (Northants) who could command a county place on leg spin alone. Warwick Tidy (Warwickshire), is a promising recruit who has not quite established himself. And there are a host of other players who bat and also bowl leg spin, either regularly or occasionally.

A leg-spinner—if he's good—may have a fair run at school. Batsmen will not be used to facing him and he will have a psychological advantage even before he comes on to bowl. News that the opposition has a good 'leggie' can turn a young batsman to jelly.

When the leg-spinner moves into club cricket he is likely to find a big difference. Many captains will regard him as an expensive luxury and bowl him at two equally unhopeful times: when the game is as good as lost and the opposition needs only a few runs to win, or when the wicket is so plumb that runs are there for the taking.

I hope the re-emergence of the leg-spinner at county level will encourage those lower down in the game. The leg-spinner, more than any other type of slow bowler, is likely to have a fight to get to the fore. He should not be disappointed if, in his early seasons in club cricket, he doesn't get much of a bowl.

Batsmen who have a bit of a feel for bowling would be well advised to experiment with leg spin. I am not suggesting they should concentrate on it to the detriment of their batting. But it's worth while trying to bowl a leg-break in the nets rather than aimlessly turning one's arm over.

Many batsmen have occasionally proved very valuable as leg-spinners. Bob Barber, fine attacking batsman that he was, was probably helped into the England side because of his leg spin. Kenny Barrington didn't need his leg spin to win him selection but it sometimes proved useful just the same.

Others still playing can tweak the ball a bit when required. Jack Hampshire (Yorkshire), 'Pasty' Harris (Nottingham), Brian Booth (Leicester), Geoff Greenidge (Sussex), and Roy Fredricks (Glamorgan) are names which immediately come to mind. The name 'Pasty' is not a misprint, by the way . . . the chap in question comes from Cornwall. Sometimes cricketers have an odd sense of humour.

Jack Hampshire seems to run through a side once every couple of years or so, which is not world-beating form but it is better than nothing. Brian Booth has occasionally taken valuable wickets for me at Leicester. Again, his tweakers are better than nothing.

During my spell as England captain I have been criticised for not favouring the inclusion of a leg-spinner in the side. It is true that when Alan Ward broke down in Australia in 1970 I preferred replacing him with another quick bowler, Bob Willis, and not with Robin Hobbs.

But that was commentary on the conditions and the make-up of the two sides, not on leg-spin bowling in general. The Australia spinners, Kerry O'Keefe, Terry Jenner and John Gleeson, never looked like winning a match and neither did Derek Underwood nor myself until the last innings of the last Test. It was not a spinners' series.

I admit that a leg-spinner can be a luxury, especially in

England. A typical attack includes a slow left-armer. If you are lucky one of your batsmen may be a Sobers or a Procter and be worth his place for both batting and bowling. Then you can juggle your eleven a little and perhaps include a leg-spinner.

But would you drop an off-spinner or a slow left-armer for a leg-spinner before a five-day Test under our unpredictable English weather? I wonder whether you would.

I have rarely cursed the fact that I've not had a leg-spinner in my side. I had no cause to do so while I was skipper in Australia, with the possible exception of the Test at Adelaide where there was a bit of lift in the wicket and a leg-spinner might have been nasty.

Also, of course, it's a question of supply and demand. Leg-spinners find it hard to win county and Test places, therefore it becomes even harder for them to win acceptance.

THE GRIP

The grip and delivery for the leg-break is slightly more complicated than those for the off-break. This time you are turning the door-knob in an anti-clockwise direction and you use the third finger (the one next to the little one) to help the spin along. You also use the wrist, and leg-spinners are therefore often referred to as wrist-spinners.

This time there is no alternative grip, as there is with the off-break. Your first two fingers have got to lie across the seam, while the third finger is wrapped under the ball so that the top joint runs along the seam. Although the little finger has little power to spin the ball, it will be placed along the seam as well.

If you sit down and flick the ball from the right hand to the left, you will find the ball spins. The more you use your wrist, the more the ball will spin. You will also find that the ball can fly out of your hand erratically.

Sometimes it will come out spinning viciously, at such an odd angle that you won't be able to catch it with the left hand. This just about sums up the young leg-spinner's life. He will be

Sweep and pull. In the two top pictures I am sweeping a ball which pitched outside leg stump. My left leg has gone towards the line of the ball and *not* inside it, to avoid being bowled round my legs; notice that my right hand is in control and turns the bat over slightly to keep the ball down. Below left, I am sweeping from outside off stump and I have put my leg in line with the ball to ensure against being bowled. Below right, note the right-hand bias to keep the ball down as I pull through mid-wicket.

Three of the world's leading batsmen. Top left, Glenn Turner (Worcestershire and New Zealand) following through with a vengeance as he approaches his tenth century of the 1970 season. Top right, Bill Lawry, the Australian opening bat, has put too much energy into this hook shot and is in danger of falling over; and, below, the poise of England batsman Colin Cowdrey after hitting to leg. His front foot is well down the wicket, yet he is perfectly balanced. You can see that the right hand has controlled the shot and therefore the ball has been kept down.

able to spin the ball a lot. His problem will be to get it to spin on a controlled path and not in any old direction.

Every leg-break bowler can be expected to bowl at least one long hop in his first over or so as he loosens up. Intikhab Alam is one of the few who can find his spot straightaway. And he is among the best leg-break bowlers in the world.

At the moment before delivery the wrist is bent outwards and is roughly parallel to the ground. The ball is released with a forward flick of the wrist which, with the leverage from the third finger, gives the ball its spin. The ball comes out of the back of the hand or almost.

As with the off-spinner, it is essential for any budding leg-spinner to spin the ball first and then worry about length and line. If you cannot spin a leg-break, there's not much point being able to pitch the ball on a sixpence because you will quickly get clobbered.

GOOGLY AND FLIPPER

A good-length leg-break is a hard ball to play. It will pitch and zip away smartly from the batsman. It might end up on the line of the off stump or outside off, perhaps forcing the batsman to snick the ball to the wicketkeeper or towards slip.

Yet an average schoolboy batsman could probably keep a top-class leg-break bowler at bay for a fair while . . . provided that the bowler had nothing but a leg-break up his sleeve. The batsman's ploy would be simple. He could shoulder his bat to most balls and stick a foot down the wicket.

It would be hard for an umpire to give him out as the ball would be turning away. The real danger would only be there if the bowler could make a ball go straight on with his leg-break action or, better still, if he could make the ball go the other way. And the good bowler can do this. The ball which goes straight on—at uneven height—is called the top-spinner or flipper; the one which goes the other way is the googly or Bosie.

E

The Bosie—this is the name the Australians use—was invented by one Bernard James Tindal Bosanquet who played cricket for Middlesex and England at the turn of the century. He was a talented games player and he experimented on a billiards table to find a way of making his leg-break bowling more effective.

He first bowled the googly in public at Lord's in 1900 and slow bowling has never been the same since. Although he played in only seven Test matches, his new and fearsome brand of delivery won two of them. On the 1903–4 tour of Australia he took six for 51 in the second innings of the fourth Test, and the next year he took eight Aussie wickets at Trent Bridge in the first Test. No wonder they call it a Bosie in Australia!

Bowling a googly is not the complicated operation it may sound. You want the ball to turn the other way, therefore you have to bowl an off-spinner; you want to fool the batsman, therefore you bowl with a leg-break grip.

The simple difference between leg-break and googly is that the leg-break is delivered out of the *side* of the hand, while the googly comes right out of the *back* of the hand and this reverses the spin. Another difference may be that the leg-break collects much of its spin from the third finger (the essential finger with some bowlers) but that for the googly this finger is, so to speak, disengaged.

The trouble with the googly is that a young bowler is likely to become obsessed with it. Once he can bowl it, there is a real danger he will regard it as his favourite toy and bowl two or three an over.

The googly's great value is its surprise element—rather like the scrum-half's break in rugby. The batsman has to be in a state of mind where he is expecting the leg-break and then . . . bang! The googly turns into him and flicks off his bat into the air on the leg-side.

Admittedly some bowlers bowl a very high percentage of googlies. Kerry O'Keefe is one. But there are leg-break *and* googly bowlers rather than simply leg-break bowlers. The googly comes so naturally to them that they will bowl it often. They do not as a rule spin the ball as much as the 'pure' leg-break bowler.

How do you spot the googly? Cricket followers will know that I am not the best batsman in the world to answer that one as I have been caught out more than once in Test matches. Against the Rest of the World at Headingley in 1970 I had reached my fifty and was going well when I shouldered my bat as Intikhab pitched outside my off stump. I played for the leg-break but it was a googly which came back and made a mess of my stumps.

I've never had much faith in the idea that you can spot the googly from the way the ball is spinning in the air. Even if you can, you will pick it up too late to play an aggressive shot. You must read the wrong 'un from the bowler's hand, which is not always easy on English grounds. The sightscreens are often poor, despite a campaign by R. Illingworth over the years.

An alternative is not to bother to spot the googly at all! This might sound foolish but I know that John Edrich, Brian Luckhurst and Basil D'Oliveira often adopt this policy. They work on the assumption that if you get to the pitch of the ball and get on top of it, it doesn't matter which way it is spinning. On the other hand if you don't get to the pitch of it, the ball must be short enough for you to see which way it turns off the pitch.

I have always preferred to try to spot the googly. It is not as difficult as it may seem. There are few top leg-spinners and you tend to play against the same ones year in year out. After a while, you get to know them better.

One clue to the googly may be that the bowler will push his left shoulder nearer to the ground with the effort of the delivery. Another is that his head will turn further over when delivering the ball.

Look at a leg-break bowler's field if you are not sure how his mind and wrist are working. Even on a good wicket, you can expect to have only three men on the leg-side. If he has his field split four-four, it could mean a number of things—it certainly means that he is unlikely to be bowling leg-breaks consistently down the line of middle-and-off.

I expect a leg-spinner to have a slip and an arc of five saving the one on the off-side for when the batsman hits with the spin. The arc begins just backward of square and contains three men in the covers, and a fairly straight mid-off. On the leg-side there will be a square leg, a mid-wicket saving one and a mid-on saving one.

This is a basic field but there will almost certainly be a variation on the off-side. Depending on where the batsman is strong, one of the three men in the covers will be pushed back to the boundary. There is little need to revolutionise this field if the wicket is helpful. The necessary changes are to move the square leg up to backward short leg and to move one of the cover fieldsmen to gully.

The leg-spinner needs bounce more than most other bowlers. Without it, his deliveries do not whip through at any pace. Therefore it seems natural enough that most of the top leg-spinners in the world today have been reared on hard wickets.

Intikhab, with whom I've had many a duel, is one of the best. He is so accurate. Leg-spinners are essentially attacking bowlers and it's rare that you will find one who can be used almost as a stock bowler. Again Intikhab is one!

Mushtaq, his fellow Pakistani, is not so accurate but he spins the ball more. Intikhab bowls a fair few googlies—there's usually one or two an over—Mushtaq does not. Mushtaq's variant is the top-spinner which pitches short of a length, hurries straight on and is liable to get you lbw.

Kerry O'Keefe is one of the latest of a long line of Australian wrist-spinners. He bowled well but not outstandingly against England in 1970–1; after he joined Somerset he adapted himself to English conditions and looked a bowler of true class although he was rather surprisingly left out of the Australian tour party of 1972.

To call him a leg-break bowler is an over-simplification. He has a leg-break (which I suspect he doesn't spin very much), a googly which he sometimes bowls half the time, and an orthodox off-break. He runs up to the wicket like a medium-pacer with a high-stepping action and brings his arm over quickly. All in all, it's a highly effective combination.

THE SLOW LEFT-ARM BOWLER

If you want to be a slow bowler, make sure you're born left-handed! This is not infallible advice but it is helpful—the slow left-armer has a natural advantage over the off-spinner and leg-spinner.

He turns the ball away from the right-handed batsman in the same way that a leg-spinner does. As this is the result of his finger-spin, he combines many of the attacking advantages of the leg-spinner with the accuracy of the off-spinner.

Normally the slow left-armer will bowl round the wicket and concentrate his attack on or about middle-and-off. The exception, in my experience, is on the third day of a match when there is some rough outside the batsman's leg stump. Then the slow left-armer can go over the wicket, pitch into the rough and have the batsman in trouble when he sweeps. I've found this sometimes pays off on the third day at Grace Road, Leicester. It might do, too, in school and club matches.

The grip for the orthodox delivery is the same as for the off-break. It is just that the picture is reversed, so to speak.

The slow left-armer can also bowl a chinaman. This is not as mysterious as it may sound—it is bowled with exactly the same action as the right-arm bowler bowls the leg-break. To the right-hand batsman, the chinaman will be an off-break.

Anyone who bowls a leg-break can also bowl a googly. Therefore the slow left-armer can pretend to bowl with a leg-break action but in fact produce a ball which goes the other way. His leg-break (or chinaman) will be an off-break to the right-hander. Therefore his googly will be a leg-break. Still with me?

The chinaman is not an important part of the modern game. Bernard Julien (Kent) bowls it when he is concentrating on his slow rather than his medium style. So do Mike Smith (Middlesex) and Barry Dudleston (Leicester) and, of course, Gary Sobers. Dudleston once got Sobers out with his chinaman . . . but he would be the first to admit that it is not an unplayable ball.

Johnny Wardle, my old Yorkshire colleague, has been the best bowler of the chinaman in England during the past twenty years. Yet he could go for two and three weeks and not bowl it; when he did, the ball would spin viciously.

Wardle bowled an excellent googly, as did George Tribe, the Australian who played for Northamptonshire. Wardle's was so hard to spot that Brian Taylor, the second wicketkeeper on the M.C.C. tour of South Africa in 1956–7, spent days on the boat trying to pick it out and still did not manage it.

All in all, Wardle was a world-class orthodox and unorthodox slow left-arm bowler. He flighted the ball excellently and —a great virtue on overseas tours—he could bowl tight on a good wicket. It is a pity that there is no comparable bowler for young players to study at the moment.

Derek Underwood (Kent) is the leading slow left-arm bowler in England. He is 28 and already has more than a hundred Test wickets in his bag. Many bowling records seem to be his for the taking. Yet to the casual observer he may look an up-and-down trundler. What has he got that is so special?

I wish I knew! There has never been anyone quite like him. He is a fine 'length and line' bowler but that is not enough. Also he bowls quickly, too quickly some would say, and at times he approaches medium pace.

One of the odd things about his bowling is that he often does not get the amount of turn you would expect. For example, he took six wickets for 12 against New Zealand at Christchurch in 1971. But he wasn't beating the bat regularly, nor was he getting very much turn. Bowling at his speed, two or three inches of turn and some bounce is enough. That is probably true of many slow bowlers; the amount of turn is often in inverse proportion to the number of wickets taken. A ball which turns almost at right angles is more likely to go for byes than to get anyone out.

Underwood is not a big spinner of the ball on a hard wicket and he relies on his accuracy to tie the batsmen down. On a wicket where he is getting some purchase, he is still not a big spinner. But he gets sharp turn and for my money he is one of the best three or four spinners in the world on a helpful track.

How good a bowler would he be if he was turning the ball into the batsman instead of away from him? That's an intriguing question. I think he might lose 30 per cent of his effectiveness.

He has tended to overshadow the other slow left-armers in England although Norman Gifford, the Worcestershire captain, returned to Test cricket against Pakistan and India in 1971. Gifford is essentially a spinner of the ball. He may get more turn than Underwood without being as accurate.

Don Wilson (Yorkshire) is a bowler who, in international terms, never quite made it. He has height, an obvious advantage, and a smooth run-up. I think his lack of success can be put down to lack of control. He has rarely been able to plug away and frustrate the batsman the way Underwood does.

There is a lesson here for young bowlers. Only one bad ball every two overs can mean the difference between dominating the batsman and being dominated by him.

Outstanding though Underwood is, he will have competition for an England place during the foreseeable future. I have already mentioned Waller of Surrey, whose career has begun brightly. Another youngster who always impresses me is David Hughes of Lancashire. The next couple of years will probably tell whether he is going to reach international class.

THINKING OUT BATSMEN

I said earlier that it was essential for a bowler—fast or slow—
to think. It is very true. Often the bowler has to con the batsman out because there is no other way. I heard a story the other
day about a lad who was starting to make the most of a plumb
wicket in a club match. He hit one ball straight over the top
and it almost carried to a small lake alongside the pavilion.

The wicketkeeper turned to slip. 'Last time anyone reached
that pool was 1946,' he said in a loud voice. 'Went on to play
for the county, the lad that did it.'

The batsman heard this and so did the bowler, an off-spinner. Before the next ball had left the hand, the batsman was
half a pace down the wicket. The bowler then whipped through
a short, faster ball wide of the off stump. The sudden change
of speed, length and line was too much for the batsman. Exit
batsman—stumped by a couple of feet. . . . As an off-spin
bowler, I wish they were all as easy as that.

But there is more than an element of truth in it. Often you
have got to persuade the batsman to get himself out and to
do this you have to play on his weaknesses: one weakness may
be his vanity.

In county cricket you come to know the strengths and weaknesses of your opponents. I've been playing against some of
them for nigh on twenty years, so if I don't know my enemy
now I never will! In schools cricket you are much more in the
dark because the other lads are likely to be complete strangers.
Even so, if you use your wits you will be able to learn a lot
about a batsman before he touches a single ball.

No one likes fast bowling and it's a fair bet that your middle-
order batsmen in schools cricket positively dislike it. It is often
a good idea to let your fast bowler have a go at a new batsman,
even if it is only for an over. I realise, though, that this is not
always possible.

As soon as the batsman arrives at the crease, look at his grip.
If he has his bottom hand underneath the handle I assume that

he will be an on-side player, that he will like the square cut, and that he won't hit too many through the covers. I would adjust my field accordingly. I would move my cover point a shade squarer, keep mid-off straight and concentrate on the mid-wicket area.

Conversely, the batsman may have his bottom hand near the top of the handle. I will assume this means an off-side bias and again this will influence my field.

This may sound elementary but I wonder how many intelligent school cricketers have ever thought of analysing a batsman in this way. You may be surprised, and your assessment may be wrong. But the odds are that you will gain an initial advantage and it will be up to your opponent to win this back.

Does the batsman move his feet? Even if he is facing quick or seam bowling you will get a good idea of how he is likely to play the spinners. He may treat the area just in front of his stumps as a minefield, and if he does it is an invitation for you to tease him with a spinner who is prepared to give the ball some air.

How does he play your spinner? His forward defensive stroke may be something of a joke . . . an instinctive lurch across the stumps with bat and pad touching one another and the bat not angled forward sufficiently. If so, you'd be foolish not to have a man waiting for the bat-and-pad at forward short leg.

There is one thing you must never do when a batsman comes to the wicket and that is mindlessly bowl at him. Whatever the score on the board you must try to grab the initiative.

Every batsman will have his weakness and it is up to you to find it. I remember when Ted Dexter came on to the scene he did not move his front foot down the wicket when playing defensively to the off-break. He left a gate, too. I used to get him out fairly often in those early days and I would expect to have an early bowl at him. After a while Dexter's foot began to move out and the gate began to vanish—he was too good a batsman to have such an obvious weakness for long.

When I use the word 'you' I am not referring only to the bowler. 'You' ought to refer to every member of the team. The wicketkeeper is particularly well placed to see what the ball is doing. Jimmy Binks was a great asset to all the Yorkshire bowlers, and he would often come up to me between overs and say: 'How about trying so-and-so . . .?' Alan Knott is the same in the England side.

Binks once told me to bowl a seamer at Clive Inman, in a match against Leicestershire. He remembered it had worked the previous year, or was it a couple of years ago? I popped in a seamer and got Inman out. It worked in the second innings too.

It pays to use your head.

6
Fielding

One of the good things to come out of the switch to one-day cricket is that this has highlighted the importance of fielding. Essex, a promising one-day side on paper, have become a first-class one because they field so well. Keith Fletcher, who used to be seen only in the slips, is often in the covers. Robin Hobbs, second only to Clive Lloyd in the outfield, will be at cover or mid-wicket. Ray East and Keith Boyce are also fast and sure, and a cut above most county fieldsmen.

Even if Essex save half a run an over in a John Player League match this adds up to 20 runs during the 40 overs. Twenty runs, as followers of the Sunday game will know, changes the complexion of a match as often as not.

The importance of fielding will become more obvious in the leagues, now that many of them are switching to limited-over matches. In school matches the value of fielding well always has—or ought to have been—blindingly obvious. Very often school sides are evenly matched. The advantages of good fielding, in terms of runs and morale, can so easily be decisive.

Professional cricketers do not have to be enticed to fielding practice in the same way that boys do, although we sometimes have the odd shilling on a contest at the slip-catching cradle. But it is a good idea to devise the occasional game to keep boys interested.

A fairly pacey one I know requires seven players. The wickets are pitched and you line up with a batsman, three cover fieldsmen (there can be two or even one), a wicketkeeper and an umpire at the striker's end, and a bowler. This bowler is, in fact, a chucker. He stands in the middle of the wicket and throws the ball to enable the batsman to make a strong hit into the covers. If the batsman hits the ball on the off and in front of the wicket, he must run two; if not, he cannot run. He can be only run out or caught.

When he is out—which will be fairly quickly—everyone moves round one. He moves to umpire to get his breath back, the umpire moves to wicketkeeper, the wicketkeeper to first-cover fieldsman and so on, with the bowler becoming the new batsman. At the end of two innings, everyone ought to feel that he has had some fielding practice.

Nearly every first-class cricketer can catch. Concentration is the main factor which sorts out the men from the boys close to the wicket. Your top-liner will expect every single ball throughout the day to be a catch; your ordinary fieldsman is prepared for a catch for, say, two-thirds of the time. Sometimes the long-suffering bowler thinks it's less!

In 1971, in the exciting Test match at Headingley, Pakistan needed 206 to win on the last day with their openers still there. In the end we scraped home by 25 runs despite a fighting 91 by Sadiq Mohammed, the youngest of the five Mohammed brothers.

I'm all for a thrilling day's cricket but this one should never have been. On the third day we dropped *six* catches as the Pakistanis fought their way to a first-innings lead.

This was bad. I know you must expect the occasional lapse but you should not expect six. However unluckily the ball may fly, you should always attain a certain standard of fielding. England got away with it on the occasion I have mentioned. Your side may not be so fortunate.

Wherever you field, there is no substitute for practice. You must practise, practise, practise. Measure the amount you practise in hours, not minutes.

CLOSE CATCHING *The slips*

The old-fashioned cradle is as good a way as any of practising slip catching. The ball flies fast and at uneven heights. Quite often the cradle will throw out a catch which beats even the swiftest slip.

The positioning of the slips always causes problems. The Australians tend to put their slips and gullies in a semi-circle and to have them so wide apart that they cannot touch hands. I can remember Bobby Simpson and Wally Grout standing way apart, so far that they would just about touch if they both dived inwards. Obviously the Aussies cover most ground this way but I would not recommend youngsters to be so ambitious.

The West Indians, on the other hand, always strike me as standing on top of one another. They look as though they could almost link arms.

The English players stand straighter than the Australians. I hope we reach a good compromise on placings during my time as captain . . . not too wide, not too close, but just right. The vital factor in deciding this is your wicketkeeper. I have told Alan Knott to go for anything he thought he could catch and this pushes first slip further round.

But a point to remember here is that the wicketkeeper will stand nearer the wicket than first slip. If he thinks a ball is not going to carry he will dive for it even if it is travelling in line for first slip; if it is travelling along the same path but carrying to slip, he may choose to leave it. Therefore it doesn't necessarily mean your placings are wrong if the wicketkeeper is diving in front of first slip—it could just be that the ball is not carrying far.

It looks bad when wicketkeeper and first slip, or two slips, go for the same ball. It's like clashing racquets with your partner at tennis. My advice to school and club players would be to risk looking silly and have wicketkeeper and slips close together. Few players at lower level are able to swallow dive around the place like the Australians.

The best slip fielder should take the first-slip position. An exception may occur when there is a good left-hand catcher in the side. The finest and fastest tickles fly either to the wicket-keeper or to the channel between him and first slip. This channel is where most chances go begging and it is an advantage if you have a left-hander who can instinctively stick out a hand there.

Whether you are fielding at first, second or third slip, it is essential to get down low and to keep low. Remember that it is easier to come up a foot to reach a ball than it is to stoop a foot.

Do not be casual about positioning yourself. Keith Miller, an outstanding Australian all-rounder of twenty years ago, used to bring off some brilliant catches close to the wicket without apparently bothering. This approach is all right . . . if you have Miller's great talent.

I think there are few worse sights—at all levels of cricket—than slips who look as though they haven't the energy to bend down and straighten up again. Occasionally you see this . . . the close fielders take their hands out of their pockets at the last minute, struggle down like a set of aged retainers and then struggle back up. This does nothing for the bowler's confidence or for the side's morale.

It is not a bad idea to make a bit of a ritual of taking up a slip-catching position. Some wicketkeepers—John Murray of Middlesex is a good example—make a similar show and it must give them a rhythm and order in their movements.

A slip-fielding drill might read: legs apart, a tug at the flannels to try to keep the creases in them, crouch low, rub the hands together, and then cup them.

First slip can and must follow the ball from the moment it leaves the bowler's hand. If he does this, and mentally plays the shot with the batsman, he will have some idea whether a catch is likely before the ball is past the bat. If he crouches there thinking about his lunch or his girl-friend, he is not going to be fielding in the slips for very long.

I do not believe there is any short cut to becoming a first-class slip fielder. You need sense and quick reactions, part of which is inborn but which is developed by the hours of practice I've mentioned. Concentration is something which is developed, too.

Physique is not important. Peter Walker (Glamorgan), the finest close catcher I've ever seen, is 6 ft 4 in and must have looked like an octopus to an impressionable young batsman. Walker was quite brilliant at either slip or leg slip and caught more catches than any other player in Glamorgan's history. In a good season he would have held between sixty and seventy.

Many were held because of the long arms which stick out from the 6 ft 4 in frame. But Walker's agility and splendid reflexes were the basic reason for his success.

Phil Sharpe (Yorkshire) and Bobby Simpson, the former Australian captain, must rank among the best half a dozen slip fielders I have seen. Neither is tall.

Sharpe is a good example of the player who has worked and worked hard to turn himself into an outstanding slip fielder. He is a beautiful catcher—especially off medium and slow bowling. Off the quicker bowling, his technique differs from Simpson's. Simpson used to catch the fast ones which came straight at him after they had rebounded off his chest. He reasoned that if he played for the rebound, it was much safer than risking missing the ball in front of his body and being unable to pick it up at the second attempt.

But the best slip catches are taken off slower bowling. When a batsman slashes at a slower ball he is likely to both change the direction and give it extra pace. The slip has only a split second in which to sight the ball. I have seen Sharpe follow the ball from a slash, be beaten by the pace, but reach behind him and take the ball after it has flown past him. That is class.

The slip fielder—and all close catchers—must know what

his slow bowler is bowling. When I first went to Leicester both the wicketkeeper, Roger Tolchard, and the first slip, Peter Marner, had trouble picking up my quicker ball. Tolchard learnt quickly but I had to tell Marner 'Third next over' (or whatever it was) so that he could take a pace backwards as I ran up to the wicket.

Gully

Fielding in the gully may seem the same as fielding in the slips but it is not. A main difference is that you cannot follow the ball as easily as first slip can. You see it reach the batsman, then you have to focus again as it comes towards you.

This is not easy. The ball can be swerving viciously as it comes off the bat. It can fall short of gully but it is much more likely to fly fast. If the batsman has put the face of the bat to the ball, it will fly faster than anything first slip is likely to get.

The gully has the advantage that he is likely to know when the ball is coming his way. The batsman will go on to the back foot or at least shape for a square drive. Even so, the fieldsman usually has all on to stop the ball.

John Edrich is one of the best gullies in the world and his fielding is an asset to any Test side. His attitude to fielding is one which every aspiring professional ought to bear in mind.

He has always been too slow over the ground to be a good Test outfielder and, although strong in the arms, his throwing is unexceptional. He has never been completely happy in the slips. That left the leg-side close-catching positions, occupied by Tony Lock and Micky Stewart for most of Edrich's early years with Surrey, and the gully . . . The gully it was.

He worked at his gully fielding. Similarly, Geoff Boycott has made himself into a valuable outfielder. The two of them have been England's most consistent run-scorers for a fair while and neither needed the 'bonus' of quality fielding to catch the selectors' eyes.

I wonder how much their fielding was worth to England

A favourite picture of my bowling action. My left leg is tense and my whole body
is pivoting on it. My arm is high and you can even see my index finger putting spin
on the ball. And, as ever, I'm sticking my tongue out in that curious way!

Leg spinner and slow left-arm. Top left, Warwick
Tidy, the young Warwickshire leg-spinner,
just before his delivery stride with his
left arm pushed good and high. Top right,
the batsman's view of Derek Underwood.
You can see from the angle of Underwood's
arms that he will pull the left arm across
his body. This arm movement, with
the front leg firm, is essential in slow bowling.
The classic way not to do it . . . Mike
Procter (Gloucestershire and South Africa)
bowls off the wrong foot. Right, a more
orthodox approach to fast bowling, although
John Snow (Sussex and England) is too
'Chest on' to the wicket to be technically correct.

during the series against Australia in 1970–1. Even if it was only 12 to 15 runs an innings, that works out at close on 150 for the whole series. Worth having.

On the leg-side

The best short-leg fieldsman I have seen? Tony Lock, Peter Walker, Peter Sainsbury, Brian Close and Peter Parfitt . . . those who know their cricket will see that all five have something in common—each is ambidextrous to one degree or another.

Lock was a right-hand bat and a slow left-arm bowler. So are Walker and Peter Sainsbury. Close and Parfitt are left-handed batsmen and right-handed off-break bowlers. If you think this is odd Mike Bissex formerly of Gloucestershire, batted right-handed, bowled left but threw right!

Close, incidentally, is a talented golfer. Playing right-handed, he whittled his handicap down to two. Then he switched to playing left-handed and again ended with a two handicap.

You need to be versatile to be outstanding close to the wicket on the leg-side. If you are ambidextrous, it helps; failing that it is an advantage if you are left-handed. Very few top-class short-leg fieldsmen are right-handed and it hard to think of one in county cricket. Dudleston and John Steele (Leicestershire), David Steele (Northants), Luckhurst (Kent), David Lloyd (Lancashire), Gary Sobers (Nottinghamshire), Gifford (Worcestershire), Amiss (Warwickshire) . . . all are left-handed or two-handed. One of the exceptions is Mike Edwards (Surrey). Another, on the face of it, was Fred Trueman. He batted and bowled right-handed. But Fred could bowl slow left-arm very accurately and that's what he was doing the first time I saw him when we were both youngsters. I was amazed when he suddenly changed his style and began hurtling them down.

Whether you are fielding in front or behind the wicket on the leg-side, you must expect to have to dive either way. Very often you find yourself going left when fielding behind.

F

Backward short-legs need the same qualities as slip and gully fielders: agility and a good eye. Those forward of the wicket or square on also need courage . . . sometimes bags of it.

In my opinion no youngster or club player should ever be made to field in a suicide position against his wishes. And no one should field there simply because he is frightened of losing face with his colleagues. That is stupid.

Wear a box if you are going to field at short-leg. If you feel you must, wear protective headgear as well. Tony Cordle (Glamorgan) set a trend in headgear in 1971 after he had seen his colleague Roger Davis hit on the chin. Without wishing to be over-dramatic, Davis is lucky to be alive. Fieldsmen can look ridiculous in crash helmets and the like but I would far rather see this than someone being helped off the field clutching his head.

Short-leg fielding has become more dangerous recently; one reason is the law which has limited the number of fieldsmen behind the wicket on the leg-side to two, the other was the 1970 lbw law. The leg-side limit was introduced to stop defensive seam bowling outside the leg stump but its main result has been to handicap slow bowlers.

The off-spinner has got to have a backward short-leg on a turning wicket. In addition he can either have a man saving one at backward square-leg or a man on the boundary. He can't have both.

So what happens when the bowler pitches one a bit short or gets one to turn slowly so that the batsman can hit with the spin? The batsman has a short-leg breathing down his neck and only one other fielder covering a vast area. He has a swing, knowing that it's odds against the man in the outfield taking a catch. And the poor chap at short-leg is in danger of getting one in the face.

The new lbw law meant the batsman could push his pad down the wicket to the off-spinner and have a free heave. Again this means danger for the chap at short-leg—pulling from outside the off stump to leg may not be textbook but it can be very effective. I can remember bowling on a turning wicket at Southampton to Barry Richards and Gordon Greenidge. They were hitting me behind on the leg-side and putting the short-legs in danger. Oh for three men behind the wicket.

Lack of bounce in first-class wickets is another factor which does not help the short-leg fieldsmen. If the wicket has bounce your short-leg fieldsmen can stand five yards from the wicket and pick up the ball off bat-and-pad. If it hasn't bounce, he has to stand that much closer.

Brian Close has stood as near to the bat as anyone I have seen. At his nearest he was not much more than a yard away. I can remember seeing a mass of bruises covering his legs after a day in the field and, of course, he is occasionally hit on the head.

Only once has he been knocked to the ground while playing cricket and that was when the batsman had a swing when Don Wilson bowled a long hop. The ball hit Close on the forehead, rebounded across the wicket and into the covers and the batsmen ran three! Close bowled the next over . . . although he said later he was seeing stars.

Men like Brian Close don't come into cricket every day. But I don't want to over-emphasise the chances of getting injured in cricket and indeed, as with some other sports, you often find that the chap who is frightened of injury is the only one who ever gets hurt. On the other hand, I would hate to think that there are players—be it 16 or 36 years of age—who are fielding short-leg on Saturdays and having nightmares from one Wednesday to the next thinking about it.

The individual knows whether he is happy fielding at short-leg. If he isn't, he should not field there. It is as simple as that.

THE MIDFIELD AND OUTFIELD

No cricket team should have to hide more than the odd fieldsman. At school level all eleven players should be reasonably mobile, even if a couple are suspect at catching. At club level you may have players who will not see 40 again and who like to bask happily at third man—but these should be the exception and not the rule. Not that age should be too important a factor. The side I took to Australia was, so many critics said, creaky at the joints. There was myself, Basil D'Oliveira and Colin Cowdrey . . . all three of us over 21.

In theory we were in for a roasting from those lithe young Aussies, who would be leaping about in the sun while we sweated. It didn't work out that way. We fielded as well as the Aussies, perhaps better.

They had a couple of brilliant covers in Paul Sheahan and Doug Walters, both of them in the best Aussie traditions. They looked like natural athletes as they moved over the ground like Neil Harvey and Alan Davidson, two Australians of earlier vintage whose fielding had this quality.

Your cover and mid-wicket fieldsman will take catches, but probably not many of them. If the batsman drives the ball correctly, the fieldsman will have no chance of a catch; if he makes a hash of the stroke, the ball is likely to fly high and present a dolly catch or go somewhere quite unexpected and defeat the fieldsmen.

This scarcity of catches does not make the role of the mid-field men less important. The value of their run-saving is hard to calculate because it can frustrate a batsman and force him into a fatal error. On the other hand, sloppy fielding keeps a batsman in good heart and demoralises the bowler.

I am sure the best cover fieldsmen are a product of natural ability plus hard work. Colin Bland, an expert at hitting the stumps after a quick pick-up, is a good example. For him, fielding became an art in itself. I can remember one occasion when rain prevented play and Bland kept the crowd entertained by throwing down the stumps from cover positions.

The experts pick up the ball and throw it as part of the same movement. Clive Lloyd (Lancashire) is a good example. His arm is already drawing back to throw the moment his fingers touch the ball. His throwing action is a whiplash. The lower part of the arm and the wrist seem to do most of the work and this, of course, speeds up the action. Often Lloyd leaves the ground as he flicks the ball. The overall effect is spectacular and exciting—Clive Lloyd at cover point is a show on his own.

Aspiring cover fieldsmen should learn to walk before they try to run. They should never be spectacular for the sake of it. Remember the basics first: keep your eye on the ball; and go down on one knee with your body behind the line to make sure the ball doesn't pop through your hands and make you look foolish. By all means try a fast pick-up if you think you have a chance of a run-out. But don't leap about the field to no purpose.

Extra cover is the run-out area—a point which both batsmen and fieldsmen should note. The bowler's end is the best target, for the obvious reason that the non-striker will have been backing up and is likely to make his ground a yard or so ahead of the striker.

Imagine a situation in which extra cover (or cover) is racing in to meet the ball and going to throw at the bowler's end. If he picks up the ball left-handed he is going to have to turn and throw the ball across his body. A right-hander is working on his natural side. Therefore your man in the natural run-out area has an advantage if he is right-handed.

Conversely, mid-wicket will be working on his natural side if he is left-handed. This division isn't strict, although it is worth bearing in mind.

I have been referring to throwing down the wicket, a tactic which some coaches may not favour. Playing according to most textbooks, one ought to throw just over the stumps at the wicketkeeper's end. The reason usually given for this is that the ball can fly anywhere after it has hit the wicket and the batsmen might run overthrows.

This is true enough, but when there is the chance of a run-out I feel it is worth shying at the stumps. The difference in time between a direct throw and the wicketkeeper breaking the wicket may be only a split second. The equivalent in distance may be only six inches. But often there is only six inches in a run-out decision.

Brian Taylor, the former Essex wicketkeeper and captain, told his fieldsmen to aim at the wicket and not at his gloves at the start of the 1971 season. It produced a rash of run-outs—23 in the first eight matches of the season. Taylor estimated that between 60 and 70 per cent were the result of direct hits. This isn't conclusive evidence, of course, but it is impressive.

There is no such thing as a specialist long-leg or third man. Often these are spots for fast bowlers because it cuts down their walking between overs. There is likely to be a fair amount of running in these positions, but there is less tension than say at slip.

This doesn't mean that you can doze off away from the front line of fire. There is always something to be learned from the men at the crease—and for all you know you might be bowling at them next over. And any player with aspirations to captaincy should be weighing the pros and cons of the state of the game. If you are continually asking yourself questions, it's a sure sign that you are never going to be chosen to provide the answers.

BOUNDARY CATCHES

A funny thing has happened to our boundary catches in the past two or three years—our time-honoured method of taking the ball has gradually been overtaken.

The traditionalists still take a skier by holding the hands cupped at eye level and by watching the ball down with the weight evenly distributed on both feet. At the moment the ball drops in, the hands go down to absorb the impetus and the elbows are automatically pushed outwards.

There are two weaknesses with this method. One is that the ball may hit the butt of the hand and bounce out. The other is that at the very last second you are liable to lose the flight of the ball as it drops out of the sky—you have been focusing on a distant object and then suddenly it is six inches from your nose.

To counteract these, many English players have adopted the Australian way of catching the high one. This is to lift the arms above the head with the palms facing upwards and with one thumb overlapping the other.

This might sound a terribly unBritish thing to do but it can be very effective. You can watch the ball right into the hands without needing to readjust your line of vision and the ball seems to stick more surely than it does in cupped hands. I have noticed at Leicester that Graham McKenzie, our Australian import, uses the hands-above-the-head method even when he is taking a running catch. That is too ambitious for English cricketers at the moment, although we may eventually desert the old way completely.

I had better make it clear that I am noting this change as something to consider, rather than recommending it as a 'must' for all schoolboys.

One definite piece of advice I would like to give to boundary fieldsmen is to avoid being too flashy. It may look splendid to throw the ball fifty yards straight into the wicketkeeper's gloves, but does it really achieve that much? The ball has spent so much time in the air that it has arrived at the wicket slowly, perhaps slowly enough to encourage the batsman to take an extra run. The most effective throw to the wicket has a near-flat trajectory and skids off the grass and into the wicketkeeper first bounce.

It is essential to throw low at the end of the day when the sun is going down, otherwise the wicketkeeper is liable to get hurt.

Also, do not expect your captain to be aware of the situation in your corner of the field. He has enough worries close to the wicket and he probably will not notice if you are two yards too fine or two square. This applies particularly to third man. Often, when batsmen are nippy, third man has to come in five yards to save the second run. He should do so on his own initiative.

The outfield used to be regarded as the place where the day-dreamers and the Billy Bunters were put in the hope that they would do as little damage as possible. Now, at senior level anyway, this has changed. In limited-over matches Kent have put their better men in the distant positions. This is logical when the match reaches the stage when wickets barely matter but runs do. Kent, particularly, appreciate what dividends there are to be gained by running between the wickets. As soon as Asif Iqbal places the ball wide of third man he is thinking of three runs.

Finally, what to do about the fast bowlers. Do you put them on the boundary between overs, realising that they may have to run but knowing that they will be mentally relaxed? Or do you put them in a close-catching position? I tend towards the idea of mental relaxation on the boundary, especially as the close-catcher is crouching and getting up again between every ball.

Fred Trueman preferred to field at short-leg, his speciality position, between overs. But his field suffered marginally during his bowling spells. A lesser player would have been better off at third man.

WICKETKEEPING

I used to keep wicket when I was in my teens. I used to enjoy it, too, because it was a sure way of staying in the game. The one thing about it I didn't like was that I couldn't bowl! Some people try to have all the fun . . .

I stopped wicketkeeping not so much because it limited my bowling chances but because of the risks of injury.

The man who convinced me was Donald Waterhouse, the Farsley skipper of that time, who, incidentally, performed the considerable feat of taking a thousand wickets in the Bradford League. He told me that I was liable to chip and break my fingers as an occasional wicketkeeper. This could mean losing a season's off-spin. It wasn't worth it.

Often the choice of a wicketkeeper in school cricket is illogical. He is usually a big lad who is put behind the wicket on the assumption that he has the bulk to get behind most of what is going.

This is bad thinking. The wicketkeeper's is the most important fielding position and as such it ought to be filled by the best fieldsman. It is so important that any consideration of a player's batting should not matter and the wicketkeeper should be chosen on his wicketkeeping ability alone.

This argument is a well-known one to Yorkshiremen because we felt for much of the sixties that we had the best wicketkeeper in the country in Jimmy Binks but that he was kept out of the England side because his batting was not good enough. You can argue about this until you are blue in the face but it proves nothing. But I have always been sure that the sensible thing to do is to go for the pure wicketkeeper.

Leaving the technicalities aside, the wicketkeeper ought to be valuable to the side as a tactician. Any side which has a wicketkeeper who doesn't study tactics is at a major disadvantage. As I hinted earlier, Jimmy Binks and Alan Knott have regularly given me valuable advice from behind the stumps.

The wicketkeeper's situation is rather like that of the goalkeeper in football. Each has got to follow the play closely for every second whether the action concerns him or not. Each ought to have the wit to appreciate things which the rest of the side cannot appreciate from its position. And each ought to tell the other players.

In practical terms, the wicketkeeper's basic priority must be to walk on the field adequately equipped. If he moves like a bow-legged duck—and we've all seen lads who do—there is something wrong. The sole reason for the wicketkeeper wearing pads is to protect his legs and knees. It is not to make him look swish. There is no reason why he should have a monstrous pair of pads: ordinary batting pads will usually do. Similarly the gloves should not be two dinner plates of waxed leather, within which it is not possible to move individual fingers. As a general rule, the newer the pads and the gloves the less effective they are likely to be. Aspiring wicketkeepers would do well to nurse their pieces of equipment over the years, to mould them into their own shape as it were.

Some wicketkeepers link the little finger of their right hand over the little finger of their left (or vice versa) so that the gloves automatically move together as a cup. I wonder how many lads can't do this because their gloves are too big and too cumbersome?

Every wicketkeeper ought to regard himself as an athlete. He should aim to be as lithe and acrobatic as any gymnast. I know this sounds suspiciously like wishful thinking. But if you want to reach the top in cricket it is ten to one that you will have to *work* damned hard to get there. This is not a game you can just turn to when rugby or football is finished.

Assuming the wicketkeeper is reasonably athletic, he should not have too much trouble when standing back to quick bowlers. He will always keep the ball in view and he will always keep his balance, being able to dive either way. The natural inclination is to edge towards leg at the moment of delivery as it is down the leg-side where the more difficult stops occur. But, as I said when talking about slip fielding, the wicketkeeper has a job to perform in front of his slips, and he will miss catches if he is worrying overmuch about leg-slide stops.

Another tendency which ought to be resisted is that of getting up too soon. Go down and stay down until you are sure it is safe to get up. If you are going to take a spectacular leg-side catch it will be by diving across from a crouching position; if you try to get up and then to fling yourself across, you will be clutching thin air.

Standing back to fast bowling should not present the young wicketkeeper with many problems. It is standing up which sorts out the men from the boys. Your reactions have to be that much faster, your reading of every ball that much more acute.

For quality keeping against slow bowling I can advise youngsters simply to watch Alan Knott. If you watch him closely you will see that for the off-spinner he will have his body inside the line of the ball and his gloves outside the line. This means that he is playing for the outside edge but that his body is well placed for a sudden switch of attention to the leg-side.

Against the slow left-armer Knott is again looking for the outside edge first, and with justification. If he catches the inside edge, it is someone's birthday.

Besides his jack-in-the-box acrobatics, I think Knott has two great assets. The first is his concentration, an essential for all close catchers. This shows towards the end of the day in a Test match, when Knott will still have all his wits about him however hard the going has been. In the seven Test matches on the tour of Australia he missed two chances. Two out of the thousands of balls he had to take! I have always been convinced that if he had been on the other side England would have lost the series instead of winning it.

Knott's other asset is his bubbling personality. Certain other great sportsmen have sparkled and it is a great aid to team morale—being a Leeds United supporter, Billy Bremner is a name which straight away comes to mind. But sticking to my own game, Godfrey Evans was another and he could inspire a side from behind the stumps in the same way that Knott can. The secret is partly in the man himself, partly in the way he does things.

Never, ever, block a return with your pads. It looks so ugly. It is a lazy way out and, as such, it dents the morale of the whole team. There is no need to be flashy. Just be cheerful, confident and as competent as you can, and you will save your side tens of runs in a day.

So much is written about Knott that it is easy to think he is the only good wicketkeeper in the world. He is not. Bob Taylor

(Derbyshire) would get into at least a couple of the other national sides on the strength of his swift moving when standing back. Farokh Engineer (Lancashire and India) is deceptively quick when he is going well.

One last name is that of Wasim Bari (Pakistan) who was so impressive when he toured England in 1971. He gets down lower than any wicketkeeper that I have ever seen with his head below the line of his pads. When Alan Knott saw this, he couldn't get over it. It is, as Alan said, an ideal position for a wicketkeeper.

7

Captaincy

Captaining a school or a club side may not be as tough as captaining a county side or England but very often it may call for considerable personal qualities. Captaincy is lovely when you are winning. When you're losing the players also can lose heart. They may have to be given a mild telling-off or even dropped. This is likely to create worries for the captain, especially if he is off-form himself.

I doubt whether the trials of captaincy become more pronounced as one goes further up the cricketing scale. I have captained England in a fair number of Tests now and have been involved in plenty of controversy, especially in Australia. But I couldn't say that leading England is any harder than leading Leicestershire.

The England captain knows that the spotlight is bang on him all the time . . . the press, television and radio see to that. A minor incident (or one which you thought was minor at the time) is liable to be chewed over again and again. Every major decision will be analysed and if the pundits think you are wrong, they won't hesitate to tell you so.

All this, however, doesn't worry me. I'm an old hand and what seems hurtful to a teenager is quite unimportant when you're thirty and over.

The England captain ought to be provided with adequate resources for every occasion. If the wicket is turning, he should be able to call on a class finger-spinner; if the ball is moving

through the air, he should have a bowler to exploit this. If he
hasn't, he and the selectors have chosen the wrong side!

The county captain is not so lucky. He may have only one
fast bowler. He may not have an accurate leg-spinner . . . although the match is crying out for one. This can be very frustrating—just as much of a strain as the pressures of Test
cricket.

HANDLING PEOPLE

There are two important elements in captaincy. One of them is
handling people in the right way, and this applies to all walks
of life; the other is tactics.

A captain must have the confidence of his players and he
has to get the best out of them; if he fails in either of these aims
he is not going to be in the job for very long. I think the way
to start players pulling with you is to realise that everyone
needs treating differently.

Geoff Boycott illustrates my point. When I first saw him
play for Yorkshire I thought he would be only an average
player. He was too content to let his runs come and he rarely
mastered the bowling.

I was wrong. He gained enough confidence to hit the ball
off the front foot and has become one of the world's top batsmen. But even when he was being acclaimed as a great player
he came up to me and asked: 'Ray, do you really think I'm a
good batsman? Or are there a lot better?'

I told him: 'You're not just a good player, you're the best.'
And I could say it with my hand on my heart. I wasn't just
boosting his ego.

Since then Boycott has had his bad spells. One of them was
in 1970 when he couldn't score runs against New Zealand. It
would have been madness to give him a roasting while he was
struggling. It was obvious that all he needed was a couple of
good scores; eventually he got them and went on to play a leading role when England regained the Ashes the following winter.

Doug Padgett is similar. He was a prodigy, playing for Yorkshire at 16, and I have always been a shade puzzled that someone of his calibre has played in only two Tests. Perhaps the reason is that he needed more than the average amount of encouragement and did not always get it.

In 1959 Ronnie Burnet, then Yorkshire skipper, gave Padgett the extra boost he needed and the result was that he scored more than 2,000 runs and had his best season.

John Snow is a different proposition. He has always bowled his heart out for me in the England team but he is a tough character and, unfortunately, both Sussex and England have had to give him a kick in the pants when he has overstepped the mark.

Ken Taylor, the former Yorkshire opener and Huddersfield Town footballer, was another player who needed the occasional gee-up. He was a natural games player and he rarely had to work hard for success. I suspect that at times he took too much for granted.

Every side will have its Doug Padgetts and John Snows. A good captain will appreciate the differences in temperament and always bear them in mind.

Similarly, the schoolmaster in charge of a team, or the club committee, will need to use their heads when they are dealing with the club captain. A schoolmaster should never use his captain as an extension of himself on the field—the lad must captain the side. Obviously he will come to the master for advice (if he doesn't, someone has picked the wrong captain) but he should not be showered with advice from first ball to last.

The relationship I have had with the England selectors has always been excellent. If there had been tension, if they spent half the day trying to dictate to me, I would have lasted for only a handful of matches.

At the end of a day's play I like to have an occasional chat with Alec Bedser, the chairman of the selectors. Notice that I say the word 'chat' because that's what it is. There is no official meeting between him and me during a match, and the captain doesn't (as some people seem to think) have to spend an hour at the end of every day's play explaining his decisions to an enraged gathering of selectors.

No, the talks I have with Bedser are quite informal. He will never offer advice, but he'll give it when I ask. This is the way it should be and it is most useful to me.

As captain I join the selectors when they are choosing a side, and this is something else I can recommend to club committees and those in charge of school sides. It is good for a young captain's morale if he has some say in the composition of the team, even if this is largely illusory. He is not likely to be effective on the field if the rest of the players regard him as the coach's lapdog.

Choosing the England side is a team effort as there must be give and take when so many possibilities are open to the selectors. I have had a very fair hearing at all meetings and no one has attempted to push a player on to me that I didn't want.

The only doubt about the final eleven has usually centred on one of the batting places and if a unanimous vote has seemed unlikely the decision has been left to me. The attitude of Bedser and his colleagues is: 'You have to go out there and captain the side. Our job is to make it as easy as possible for you.' It is an attitude which has worked very well.

READING THE WICKET

Judging a wicket correctly must be one of the hardest things in the world. I have been at it for twenty years and I must suppose that I have an astute cricket brain. I do now get the answer right about 90 per cent of the time, but sometimes I am almost guessing. There is usually a chunk of intuition mixed in with my reasoning as I gaze down at the strip and try to work out what it will do.

Always carry a ball with you when you go to look at a

Alan Ward (Derbyshire and England) in flight . . . a picture which sums up the athleticism and balance of fast bowling. It's an art all right.

Gary Sobers, hitting straight and on the up—the type of shot which makes him, to my mind, the best cricketer in the world.

wicket. Try to bounce it fairly firmly near the block hole (or anywhere where you will not be denting the surface) and note the result. If the ball bounces two feet or more, you are going to be playing on a pacey wicket; if it barely rises back off the ground, the wicket will be slow.

Of course, we are talking about loose yardsticks already. Just how firmly is 'fairly firmly'? That is difficult to answer and only experience will finally tell you.

Even if you are not the captain, it is worth while trying this bouncing test on a wicket. And start next match, not in ten years' time when you think you might be captain of your club side. Start building up your case history of how wickets behave because you are never too young to learn.

The bounce will tell you something, and so will the appearance of the grass. And in England you are likely to find that the wicket will fall into one of four categories:

1 a hard surface which is well knit together (without cracks, of course!) and which has a cushion of green grass on it.

2 a surface which is again hard and firm but on which the grass is a straw or brown colour.

3 very little grass on this one as most of it has been shaved away, but you can see plenty of grass roots binding the soil together.

4 even less grass here, and the surface is almost like baked mud.

The first type ought to be made for fast bowlers. It should have pace and bounce, and the seam of the ball should deviate off the green grass. If the atmosphere is at all heavy, enabling the ball to move in the air, the side batting first is likely to be in deep trouble. This type of wicket is reminiscent of Lord's up to the early sixties. Throw in the Lord's ridge, and it makes me wonder how anyone ever scored runs on that track.

Type two—with the brown or straw-coloured grass—is liable to be pacey with the new ball. But it will not seam. As there is little juice or moisture, the surface is liable to break a little—how quickly will depend on the weather.

G

Type three is likely to be a deceptive one. It might look as though it will break up but it won't. I can remember captain after captain and spinner after spinner waiting for the Trent Bridge pitch to break up. It didn't because the roots held the surface together. The spinners managed a little direction-change late in the match and that was all.

In England type four—the baked mud—ought to turn by the second day because there is nothing to stop the surface crumbling once the fast bowlers begin thumping the ball on to it. A number of the minor grounds used to have pitches similar to this, but the only one I play on these days is the college ground at Cheltenham, which invariably turns before the third day.

Many a captain must have gone overseas and seen a baked mud strip in India and Pakistan, whispered a quiet 'eureka' to himself, and put his faith in his spinners. And he will have been disappointed, for Gloucestershire mud is not Ganges mud. Much of the soil overseas has binding qualities foreign to us: you can play on some of it for a week and it will be as firm as ever.

Nowadays I find overseas wickets hardest to judge. For instance, you can find that your firm and true strip, which is allegedly made for fast bowlers, will turn for three or four hours on the first day! The reason is that there is damp underneath which is quickly sucked upwards. Perth used to be like this, although there was no way of telling whether there was moisture underneath or not.

I have misjudged Perth in the past and I have even misjudged my own pitch at Leicester. I can remember one occasion when Jack Birkenshaw, my fellow off-spinner, and I were flexing our fingers as rain freshened up a track which looked short of grass. We were both convinced it was going to turn. But there was more grass on it than we thought and the ball skidded off it instead of turning.

I have only twice put in a side in a Test match. The first was at Melbourne in 1971. Not a ball was bowled. I did it

again against Australia at Trent Bridge in 1972. The weather
was perfect and there was every indication the sun would last
for another week. Experience of Trent Bridge, a study of
Nottinghamshire results that season and a close look at the
wicket convinced me it would play easier and better as the
match progressed.

I thought the best chance of winning the match would be
to give my bowlers first use of the wicket when it had some
'life' in it. As it happened, the match was drawn and England
had no trouble in surviving the whole last day. We did not make
the breakthrough I wanted on the first day because three or
four sharp chances did not stick otherwise Australia might
easily have been bowled out for around 200 instead of the 315
they reached.

On other occasions I have thought about batting second in
England but on each occasion the weather forecasters have
dissuaded me. However uncertain the conditions have been at
the start, I have thought that they would get worse if the
expected rain arrived and that it was better to bat first and try
to get to, let us say, 100 for three, before the first downpour.
Unfortunately the forecasters have let me down more than
once.

PACING A GAME

Tactics begin the moment you shout 'heads' or 'tails' and the
coin spins in the air. They end in the bar when the match is
won or lost, with some chap telling you that you handled the
bowling wrong, set bad fields, ought to have changed the batting order . . . and so on and so on.

What if you win the toss? Whether to bat or not is a
question which has been thrown into the melting pot in
league cricket in the past couple of years because of the switch
to the over-limit game. Previously I think it was fair to say that
most captains batted if they won the toss: given a good start,
one could then expect to dominate play throughout and time

a declaration. Now, with each side having a set number of overs, there is a feeling that the side batting second 'knows how quick it's got to go'.

My advice to captains winning the toss in minor cricket is simple. It is *bat*.

Let's suppose you are playing in a 40-over match and you bat first. If your team scratches about at the wicket like a set of maiden aunts and you are bundled out for 80 or less, it's odds on you are going to lose and would have lost if you had batted second.

But if you get runs, even if it is at no more than three an over, it will mean that a good captain and good bowlers can manipulate the situation and they retain an advantage over the team batting second.

If you have set the opposition 121 to win, you know you must bowl your spearheads from the word go, hoping to cut down the runs and get wickets. There is no point in giving your best seamer three overs and then replacing him with a trundler. You have got to break through early on, otherwise you have lost. If the opposition is trying to get 181 to win, the situation is different. Your trundler, who never gets anyone out, is much more valuable because the onus is on the batsman—he has got to get runs fairly fast. In this case you are more likely not to overbowl your best seamer at the start but to save some of his firepower for the point about the twentieth over when the batsman will have to accelerate.

It is a different story again if the score is 221. If you choose, you can defend from the outset and be in little danger of defeat. Better still, you can probably give your spinners a good bowl. This is a move which can demoralise the opposition: it can be relatively easy to maintain a certain scoring pace against medium-pacers, flicking a ball here and tickling one there, but it's not nearly so easy to score five or six runs an over off an accurate spinner.

Of course, there are refinements to the basic pattern. A good captain will sense the crisis points during the opposition innings: the time when they are in the ascendant and looking dangerous; the time when they are looking lost and when one breakthrough will almost certainly defeat them, and so on.

As a counter to these, the captain can change either his bowling or his field. He can slow down the physical pace of the match, too. I think it is a quite fair tactic in a match when both sides receive the same number of overs. It is natural for a bowler to walk back to his mark with plenty of zest if he's taking wickets, and with not so much zest when he's getting clobbered. This is reflected throughout the side as a whole. I consider it reasonable for the captain to have that extra word with his bowlers between overs when the going is bad. He will tend to change his field more, too. He ought to try anything (within the spirit of the game, of course) which will upset a batsman in full flow.

Get some runs in the bank in your 40 overs or so and you are in the box seat. Bat second and life is not so easy.

Similar advice usually applies to three- and five-day matches. *A good captain, it's sometimes said, always thinks about putting the other side in and then always bats.* Occasionally you see an obvious early advantage in putting the other side in, usually when there is moisture in the wicket which will dry out on the first day. Even then you have to weigh this advantage against the disadvantage of batting fourth.

There are so many different types of limited-over matches nowadays that some time soon a captain is going to make the mistake of pacing his innings expecting 60 overs and finding that there are only 40.

I was given plenty of time to ponder the ins and outs of cricket. I was in my eighth season in the three-day game before I played in a Test. Then it was another five years before the 60-over Gillette competition came into being, to be followed by the John Player League. Today a young player who makes a quick rise to the top will find himself playing in *five* different types of cricket within a couple of seasons: that is, the three one-day competitions, the championship and Tests.

At the start of 40-over matches, some captains did find themselves miscalculating. They found that their quick bowlers bowled the 39th over, but still had one of his eight left. The upshot has been that captains for a long time have tended to give bowlers spells of an even number of overs!

One of the minor benefits of the new competitions has been that captains have found it much easier to switch batting orders around and to experiment. In the three-day game batting orders have been sacrosanct to players for little reason. A number four is going to bat in very different circumstances from match to match—once after half an hour with the score at 12 for two, the next time after five hours with 250 for two on the board.

But for purely psychological reasons batsmen on the whole wish to bat in one particular position. Clive Inman disliked moving from the number four spot for Leicestershire; Brian Davison likes the number five spot. I can understand this although it isn't really much more than superstition. I hope that club and junior sides will keep their batting orders fluid from the outset. It is easier for a captain when he can switch an order straight away and not feel as though he is breaking a hallowed tradition.

One occasion on which I am dubious about switching the order is when a nightwatchman is traditionally called on. Without going into all the pros and cons, I feel that using a nightwatchman is almost exclusively a Test-match tactic these days. Only if the light is bad and the opposition is on top at 40 for three (or worse) is it worth while using a nightwatchman.

It is when you use a nightwatchman in a county match that you can often come unstuck. For a start, a Test number seven, eight or nine, ought to be able to stick it out for a few minutes when promoted. But your county player is liable to get himself out and make you look a fool. At the other extreme, he will stay there and go in next morning with the sun shining and the whole state of the game changed. You want him to score a quick twenty and then get out to make way for an established batsman. Unless carefully instructed he may stay there for eighty minutes while scraping ten or eleven together and giving the innings no momentum at all. A few years ago this wouldn't have mattered overmuch. Now, with bonus points, it is serious —you can lose two or three points if the innings sags at the wrong time.

PUTTING YOURSELF ON

Captains tend to be batsmen rather than bowlers, which has always struck me as being a trifle odd. There is no earthly reason why the captain should not be a bowler and the old argument about a bowler 'not knowing when to take himself off' is so much rubbish.

I have often been criticised for not bowling myself enough as England and Leicestershire skipper. I expect other bowler-captains have been similarly criticised (or been told they are bowling too much!)

My advice to any captain whose role in the side is being criticised is: analyse your position as sensibly and dispassion-ately as you can and then do what you think is best. Don't get in a lather because some barrack-room lawyer in the side thinks you always put yourself on at the best end.

My case is fairly instructive. I think it's a good case of people criticising the captain when they don't know, or don't appreci-ate, all the facts.

One obvious factor which restricts my over total in a season is that I'm playing in five or six Test matches. I play in fewer matches than, say, Fred Titmus and furthermore one tends to bowl fewer overs in Tests.

Reason two is that there are other people in the Leicester-shire side who sometimes need a bowl more than I do. We have a first-class spinner in Jack Birkenshaw, and if it's obvious that we slow men are going to get only a few overs, I'd rather Jack bowled them.

Even if he doesn't get a wicket, he's made a contribution to the side which is good for his confidence. I don't need this boost. I'm captaining the side anyway and trying to build up a team for the future—and I certainly don't need to bowl a few overs to show my friends in the press box that I can still do it.

In minor cricket the pressures are not so great. Even so I think the young player who is captaining in a competitive match should stick to his guns when it comes to bowling himself and deciding on field placings and the batting order. Don't be afraid to take decisions.

SOME OUTSTANDING CAPTAINS

The best captain I have ever played under is Richie Benaud. He led only one tour to England—in 1961—and the Aussies took home the Ashes, winning two matches to our one.

Looking back on that tour, the Aussies had no right to win. We had a strong middle order with Ken Barrington batting at either five or six, and an opening attack of Fred Trueman, who won the Headingley Test almost on his own, and Brian Statham. But the decisive factor was Benaud's captaincy. He always had a magnificent gift of making his players feel ten feet tall. If the Aussies had given 100 per cent in 1961, they might still have lost. Benaud dragged 105 per cent out of them.

It is hard to say how, although I had first-hand experience of his leadership when he took a Commonwealth team on a six-week tour of South Africa in 1961. He had bags of personality and an infectious enthusiasm. If I didn't think I was going to get a man out he soon changed my mind for me.

'You can do this fellow,' he'd come up and say. 'How about a couple of short-legs?'

Benaud was always ready to attack, to put men up around the bat, but he would never go tilting at windmills for the sake of it. The pressure would always come at the right time and have the maximum effect.

From Benaud, who was every inch a pro, to Ronnie Burnet,

a pure amateur. Who? I can hear the non-Yorkshiremen ask, and it's a fair question. Burnet wasn't a first-class cricketer and he became Yorkshire skipper in 1958 at the age of 39. During his first season Yorkshire had dropped from third to eleventh in the championship, and three former Test players, Johnny Wardle, Bob Appleyard and Frank Lowson weren't re-engaged.

The next year Yorkshire won the championship, the start of a golden run during the sixties. I doubt whether it would have happened without Ronnie Burnet.

His secret was that he treated everyone very, very fairly whether he took to them personally or not. He understood that certain players needed a quiet word of encouragement, others needed jogging along. He was always ready to ask advice from the professionals and he realised his own technical limitations.

We all knew that the other ten were virtually carrying him as a player and he was sensible enough not to make excuses for his cricket. But there were no sly remarks if the skipper came back to the dressing room with nought against his name, because we all respected him and saw that he was starting to build a new spirit in the side.

No one would put Burnet among his all-time greats. But he did a heck of a lot for Yorkshire—and they reaped the dividend for ten years.

Although there are no amateurs in cricket now, there are still times when the 'gifted amateur' can be very useful in leading a side. One proviso, though . . . in these days of one-day cricket you can't afford to carry anyone in the field. A couple of dud fielders can cost you 40 runs. Your gentleman player must be reasonable in the field, even if he holds the bat at the wrong end.

Much of the credit for Surrey's golden run in the fifties must go to their captain, Stuart Surridge. He was a better cricketer than Ronnie Burnet, being a useful seamer who could tonk a few runs and a fine close fieldsman. His main job, though, was to skipper the side. He, too, had the knack of getting the best out of his men. He would humour and encourage Jim Laker, who could suddenly lose heart and enthusiasm, and a moment later he would be blasting Tony Lock, a flamboyant character.

Now to England. I played under Norman Yardley, a former England skipper, for Yorkshire in the early fifties. Norman was very good technically but I found him too nice. He was reluctant to give someone a kick when he deserved it.

Len Hutton had a reputation for being a bit dour and this was probably deserved, although he often had to carry England's batting *and* he also had the burden of being England's first professional captain in modern times. I thought his fault was that he was too 'fast bowler conscious'. He'd faced all kinds of bowling, decided which he liked the least, and went for that when he was skipper.

Peter May, well liked by his players and not short of personality, was the best England captain I came into contact with. He was an amateur with a professional approach and not the type to compromise or accept second best. Perhaps this was the result of his history—he had learnt his captaincy under Stuart Surridge and Len Hutton.

Of the more recent crop of county captains, Brian Close is near the top of everyone's tree because of his immense knowledge of the game, his courage and aggression.

Five of the seventeen first-class counties began the 1971 season with new captains. And, not to mince words, three of them were replacing men who had been sacked. It is no easy job being a captain, as the resignation of Mickey Stewart—subsequently withdrawn—confirmed in the same season.

When the season was about half gone, Stewart, the Surrey captain, announced he was going to resign at the end of the season after nine years. The reasons he gave were a bit frightening. He said he was sleeping only four hours a night . . . he was beginning to snap at his wife and children . . . he wasn't enjoying his cricket any more . . . and he guessed that the captaincy was costing him 600 runs a season.

Quite a catalogue, isn't it? It becomes a bit frightening when you realise that Stewart would have been near the top of anyone's list of county captains No one was gunning for him, and at the time he was intending to resign Surrey were starting the surge which brought them the championship.

I rated Stewart almost as good a leader as Close. He had a happy-go-lucky air on the field but he could gee on a side well enough when the occasions arise. Glancing through the record books I see to my surprise that he never won anything in the nine years he led Surrey, with the exception of the championship in 1971.

Which reminds me of another thing a captain has to be . . . successful.

Like every other member of his team, a captain must work really hard at his game. In this way he will earn the respect of his players and get the most out of cricket. Like me he may learn to love cricket as the most fascinating game of all.

8

Knowing the Language

Cricket has a language of its own, rather like motor cars and the hi-fi industry, which often means that wives and girl-friends wander to the other side of the room when the men start talking cricket. While it is pleasant to have a vocabulary of one's own, I suppose there is a slight danger that the youngster may be driven away by all the strange terminology. If so, I hope the following definitions (by no means exhaustive) will help:

anchor man: a batsman who stays at the wicket, venturing little in order to prop up the innings, while the chap at the other end scores the runs.

backlift: the withdrawal of the bat backwards before playing a stroke. The majority of top batsmen have a generous backlift. Exceptions are Brian Luckhurst, John Edrich and especially Basil D'Oliveira.

beamer: a full-pitched ball which a batsman finds coming at his head to intimidate him. It is a fast bowler's weapon, of course, and rarely effective.

bodyline: a term we don't hear too often these days, thank goodness! It was the name given to the intimidatory, short, leg-side fast bowling with which Harold Larwood and Voce subdued and beat the Australians in 1931–2. In a modern context it simply means fast bowling which arrives about waist to head high.

bosie: the Australian name for the googly, the ball which

looks from the bowler's action like a leg-break, but which in
fact turns from off to leg.

bottom hand: the right-hander holds the bat with the left hand
above the right. The left should dominate the majority of
strokes; if the right does, the batsman is said to 'bottom
hand' the ball away.

bouncer: a ball which a fast bowler pitches short of a length
so it rears up near the batsman's head.

castle: the stumps (colloquial).

cherry: the new ball (colloquial).

chinaman: normally the left-arm spinner will turn the ball
away from the right-handed batsman, that is towards the slip
or slips. The chinaman is the ball he turns the
other way.

Chinese cut: a snick which doesn't go where the batsman
intends. Usually it flies uncomfortably near the stumps off
the inside edge and towards fine leg.

cutter: a quick ball which deviates off the wicket because the
seam gets purchase.

daisy cutter: a ball which keeps low; often called a grub in
Northern playgrounds.

drag: the fast bowler's action of dragging his back foot over
the crease which caused umpires trouble until the no-ball rule
was changed and the front foot became the vital one.

duck: as plonger; no score.

Duke of Spain: rain. But I've no idea of the derivation. Must
be cockney rhyming slang.

finger-spinner: a bowler who spins the ball with his index
finger, that is from off to leg if he is right-handed.

flier: not a speedy cover point but a wicket of doubtful quality
from which the balls rear at uneven heights.

flipper: a leg-break bowler's ball which has top spin on it and
which hurries through at uneven height. If he gets a wicket,
it is often lbw.

gate: the area between the bat and pad, through which the
batsman should never be bowled.

googly: a ball which looks from the bowler's action as if it is a leg-break, but which in fact turns off to leg.

grippers: another name for the slips.

guard: the point on the crease in relation to the stumps where the batsman aligns his bat.

gully: a close catcher who is behind, but only just behind, the wicket on the off-side. He will take the ball which the batsman hits just behind square while the slips will take the accidental tickle.

Harrow drive: a shot which goes in an unexpected place. (Sometimes called a Chinese cut.)

hob: to 'hob' means to 'castle' or bowl out; another expression which, I suspect, is heard frequently north of the Trent.

hook: the attacking shot played to the bouncer which, if you are fortunate, sends the ball somewhere over square-leg for six.

inswinger: the ball which swings through the air and moves from the batsman's off towards leg.

jack: the number eleven batsman, so-called because of the card sequence of nine, ten, jack.

king pair: being out first ball twice in a two-innings match.

length: a term which often foxes learned cricketers but shouldn't. A length ball is one which pitches at such a point that the batsman cannot go forward or backwards with any certainty.

long hop: a ball of bad length, one that pitches so short of the batsman that it hops pleasantly towards him and gives him an easy, swinging hit.

long leg, long off and long on: is the long leg the one in front of the wicket or behind? Long off and long on are both in front of the wicket and on their respective sides of it. Long leg is behind.

Nelson: Admiral Nelson had one eye and one arm and Nelson in cricket is all the ones—111 for a side or an individual. Double Nelson is 222.

nightwatchman: a low-order batsman who is promoted late

in the evening to avoid a more valuable batsman risking his wicket during the final few minutes.

outswinger: the ball which swings through the air and moves from the batsman's leg to his off-side.

pair: no-score twice in the same match. Slightly less embarrassing than a king pair but quite bad enough.

plonger: slang term for scoring no runs.

point: fielding position square of the wicket on the off-side which has now gone out of favour.

runner: a colleague who runs for a batsman who is injured and cannot run for himself. He will stand at square-leg when the injured batsman has the strike and at the bowler's end at other times.

sightscreen: the white screen or painted area behind the bowler which enables the batsman to pick up the arm as it comes over. The sightscreens on most English first-class grounds are bad.

silly point; silly mid-on and silly mid-off: a 'silly' position is one which looks and often feels too close to the bat for comfort.

slip: see gully. The slips stand straighter than the gully, forming the arc between them and the wicketkeeper.

sticky wicket: a phrase which cricket has given to the language. It is a wicket which is damp and breaking up from which the ball spins viciously. The true sticky wicket needs a certain type of soil found in South-east Asia and Australia but not, I believe, elsewhere. But the phrase is applied to English wickets just the same.

stonewalling: as you would expect, dour and unambitious defence from a batsman.

sundries: the Australian term for extras—that is the wides, byes and no balls which go to the batting total but do not come from the bat.

sweep: shot played with a semi-circular move of the bat across the line, usually against slow bowling.

ton: a century (colloquial).

wrist-spinner: the finger-spinner uses his fingers to bowl off-breaks, the wrist-spinner uses fingers and wrist to bowl leg-breaks and googlies.

wrong 'un: colloquialism for the googly.

yorker: a ball of full length which the bowler tries to get under the bat, usually as the batsman comes forward a little. It is normally associated with fast bowlers but is also a good surprise weapon for a slow bowler.